LANDMARKS AND SURFACE MARKINGS
OF THE HUMAN BODY

RAWLING'S LANDMARKS AND SURFACE MARKINGS OF THE HUMAN BODY

NINTH EDITION

REVISED BY

J. O. ROBINSON, M.D., M.Chir., F.R.C.S.

SURGEON, ST. BARTHOLOMEW'S HOSPITAL, LONDON
FORMERLY DEMONSTRATOR OF ANATOMY, ST. BARTHOLOMEW'S HOSPITAL.

WITH THIRTY-EIGHT ILLUSTRATIONS

LONDON
H. K. LEWIS & Co. Ltd.
1973
(Reprinted)

First Edition	.		.	.	.	1904.
Second Edition	.		.	.	.	1905.
Third Edition	.		.	.	.	1908.
Fourth Edition	.		.	.	.	1911.
Fifth Edition	.		.	.	.	1912.
Reprinted	.		.	.	.	1914.
,,	.	.	.	.	.	1916.
,,	.	.	.	.	.	1918.
,,	.	.	.	.	.	1918.
,,	.	.	.	.	.	1920.
,,	.	.	.	.	.	1920.
,,	.	.	.	.	.	1922.
Sixth Edition	.		.	.	.	1924.
Seventh Edition			.	.	.	1929.
Reprinted			.	.	.	1932.
,,	.	.	.	.	.	1935.
,,	.	.	.	.	.	1937.
Eighth	.		.	.	.	1940.
Reprinted			.	.	.	1942.
,,	.	.	.	.	.	1944.
,,	.	.	.	.	.	1946.
,,	.	.	.	.	.	1948.
Ninth Edition	.		.	.	.	1953.
Reprinted	•		.	.	.	1958.
,,		.	.	.	.	1963.
,,		.	.	.	.	1967.
,,		.	.	.	.	1973.
,,		.	.	.	.	1980.

©

H. K. LEWIS & CO. LTD.

1958

I.S.B.N. 0 7186 0161 0

Made and printed in Great Britain by
Adlard & Son Ltd., Bartholomew Press, Dorking

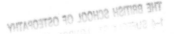

PREFACE

The correction of a few errors is all that has been found necessary in revising the ninth edition. Surface markings and measurements have been defined in fairly strict fashion with the object of making their learning an easier task. The reader is asked to appreciate that there is considerable variation in the human body and that only an average representation has been chosen. It should also be stressed that the living is a far better subject from which to learn than any cadaver.

James O. Robinson.

London, S.W.1.

PUBLISHER'S NOTE TO THE NINTH EDITION

The first edition of Rawling's Landmarks appeared in 1904, and several of the subsequent editions have been reprinted as occasion demanded. The eighth edition was published in 1940 and no fewer than four reprints have been made. As it is apparent that the book remains acceptable to the student, it was considered it might be revised with advantage. Consequently a copy was submitted to Mr. Robinson, of St. Bartholomew's Hospital, who kindly looked through it, and he has made a few minor alterations to the Text which were all that were thought necessary. In addition, however, the Section on Ossification and Epiphyses of the skeleton has been extended and several new illustrations have been appended.

CONTENTS

CHAPTER I

ILLUSTRATIONS

LANDMARKS AND SURFACE MARKINGS OF THE HUMAN BODY

CHAPTER I

THE HEAD AND NECK

CRANIO-CEREBRAL TOPOGRAPHY

ONLY those landmarks and surface markings will be given which are of practical value, and, as far as possible, each landmark will be rendered independent of any other, as by such means any given structure can be rapidly depicted on the surface, the important question of time and of space rendering the more complicated systems, in which it is necessary to map out a network of intersecting lines in order to fix the position of any single structure of little surgical value. It is necessary, however, to recognize first certain important bony points, etc.

The *nasion*, situated at the base of the nose at the central point of the naso-frontal suture.

Fig. i, 1.

The *inion*, or *external occipital protuberance* —a projection, variable in size, which can be felt on the occipital bone, immediately above the nuchal furrow.

Fig. i, 2.

A line uniting these two points over the vertex of the skull corresponds in direction to the *longitudinal fissure of the brain*, to the upper attached margin of the *falx cerebri* and to the *superior sagittal venous sinus*. This sinus originates in the region of the foramen cæcum, just anterior to the crista galli of the frontal bone, broadening out as it passes backwards to the internal occipital protuberance, which corresponds, on the outer aspect of the skull, to the inion. The sinus then turns sharply to

I

the right, forming the right *transverse sinus*. The left sinus derives its blood mainly from the *straight sinus*, which receives, at the anterior margin of the tentorium cerebelli, the great cerebral vein (Galen) and the inferior sagittal sinus which is contained in the free margin of the falx cerebri. The line, drawn as above from the nasion to the inion, also corresponds in direction to the occasionally persistent *metopic* suture between the two halves of the frontal bone, and to the *sagittal* suture between the two parietal bones.

The frontal bone is separated off from the two parietal bones by the *coronal* suture, and the point of junction of the coronal and sagittal sutures is known as the *bregma*, the site of the fœtal anterior fontanelle, an opening which should be closed before the end of the second year. Between the parietal and occipital bones the *lambdoid* suture lies ; and at the junction of the sagittal and lambdoid sutures the posterior fontanelle is situated, closed at or soon after birth. The point of **Fig. i, 13.** junction of the last two sutures is known as the *lambda*. This point lies about 2½ inches above the inion or external occipital protuberance. About 1 inch from its posterior superior angle, and close to the sagittal suture, the parietal bone is perforated by a small foramen —the parietal foramen—for the transmission of an emissary vein. A line uniting the two foramina crosses the sagittal suture at a point known as the *obelion*. The parietal bone is outwardly bulged at a point **Fig. i, 11.** rather above its centre, forming the *parietal eminence*—this is more pronounced in the fœtal skull, and indicates the point at which the single ossific nucleus makes its appearance.

Turning now one's attention to the lateral aspect of the

Fig. i, 6.   skull, the *temporal lines* should be examined. They are two in number, superior and inferior, crossing the parietal bone rather below the junction of the middle and lower thirds, cutting off the vault proper above from the temporal fossa below. The ridges are often so feebly developed in this region that it may be necessary to verify their position by tracing them backwards from the zygomatic process of the frontal bone, at which level the upper line is always well marked. The temporal muscle arises from the inferior temporal line and from the temporal fossa below, whilst the overlying fascia, the tem-

Fig. i, 5.   poral fascia, gains attachment to the *superior temporal line*—a feebly developed ridge which runs above and parallel to the inferior line.

The *zygomatic process of the frontal bone* articulates with

Fig. ii, 16.   the corresponding process of the zygomatic bone, and the articulation between the two processes is easily felt at the upper and outer border of the orbital cavity.

The *marginal tubercle*, a small prominence to be felt

Fig. i, 12.   along the posterior border of the frontal process of the zygomatic bone, a short distance below the fronto-zygomatic suture.

The *zygomatic process* of the temporal bone should be traced backwards towards the ear, and an examination of the skull will show that this process divides in front of the ear into three roots, the anterior merging into the articular eminence, the middle helping in the formation of the post-glenoid tubercle, whilst the posterior or upper

Fig. ii, 13, 14.
Fig. i, 17.   root sweeps backwards above the external auditory meatus to become continuous with the suprameatal and supramastoid crests, and to blend with the posterior curved end of the temporal line.

The *suprameatal crest* is of special surgical importance, as it forms the upper boundary of Macewen's suprameatal triangle (aural operations), and also indicates fairly accurately the lower level of the cerebrum in this situation.

The *transverse sinus*.—Draw a band, ½ inch in width,

Fig. i, 16.   from the inion, or external occipital protuber-
Fig. ii, 9.   ance, to a point ¾ inch behind the external auditory meatus, so curved that the highest point of the convexity lies about ¾ inch above Reid's base-line.

The *lower limit of the cerebrum* can be mapped out in

Fig. i, 17,   the following manner :   A point is taken in the
17, 17.   median antero-posterior line about ½ inch above the nasion, and from this point a line is drawn outwards which lies about ½ inch above, and follows the curve of the upper border of the orbit. This line is carried backwards as far as the level of the zygomatic process of the frontal bone, then curving upwards and backwards towards the *pterion* (see next page). The temporo-sphenoidal lobe now sweeps downwards and forwards towards the posterior border of the zygomatic bone, and then lies practically on a level with the upper border of the zygomatic process of the temporal bone. At and behind the ear the cerebrum lies flush with the suprameatal and supramastoid crests, and subsequently follows the curve of the transverse sinus from the base of the mastoid process to the external occipital protuberance.

The transverse sinus is, to a large extent, walled in by the *tentorium cerebelli*, a membrane separating the cerebrum above from the cerebellum below. The *sinus curve*, therefore, corresponds not only to the position of the transverse sinus, but also represents the outer attachment of the tentorium cerebelli, and the interval between the cerebrum above and the cerebellum below.

Reid's base-line.—A line is drawn backwards from the

FIG. I.

1. The nasion.
2. The inion.
3. The mid-point between nasion and inion.
4. The central sulcus (fissure of Rolando).
5. The superior temporal line.
6. The inferior temporal line.
7. The pterion.
8. The anterior horizontal ramus of the lateral cerebral sulcus (Sylvian fissure)
9. The anterior ascending ramus of the lateral cerebral sulcus.
10. The posterior ramus of the lateral cerebral sulcus.
11. The parietal prominence.
12. The marginal tubercle of the zygomatic bone.
13. The lambda.
14. The superior temporal sulcus.
15. The parieto-occipital sulcus.
16. The transverse sinus.
17, 17, 17. The level of the base of the cerebrum.
18. The external auditory meatus.
19, 19. Reid's base-line.

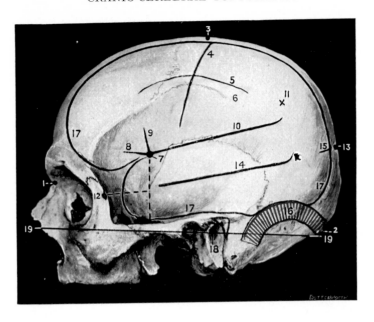

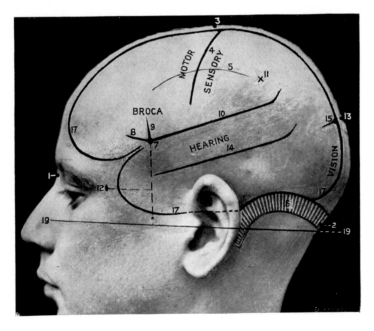

FIG. I.

To face p. 4.

FIG. II.

1, 1. Reid's base-line.
2, 2. A line parallel to the above at the level of the supra-orbital margin.
3. The middle meningeal artery.
4. The anterior branch.
5, 5, 5. The three sites for trephining.
6. The posterior branch.
7. The site for trephining.
8. The point for trephining to reach the inferior cornu of the lateral ventricle.
9. The transverse sinus.
10. The inion.
11. The mastoid process.
12. Macewen's suprameatal triangle.
12a. The tympanic antrum.
12b. The facial nerve.
13. The suprameatal and supramastoid crests.
14, 14. The temporal line.
15. The temporal fossa.
16. The zygomatic process of the frontal bone.
17. The site of attachment of the medial palpebral ligament (tendo oculi).
18. The lacrimal groove.

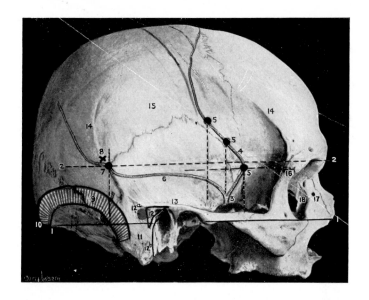

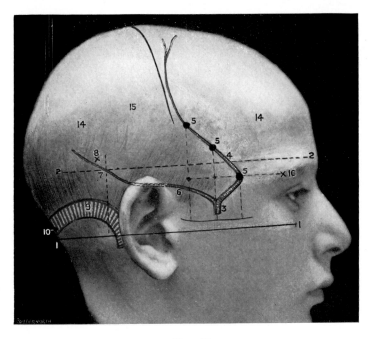

FIG. II.

To follow Fig.

Fig. i, 19,
19.
Fig. ii, 1, 1.
lower border of the orbit to the middle of the external auditory meatus, and, when further produced, the line will be found to fall just below the level of the inion, and to lie almost entirely below the level of the transverse sinus. This line is utilized by some surgeons in trephining the skull, distances being measured along this line and points taken above or below, according to the seat of the lesion.

The Sylvian point represents the site of divergence of
Fig. i, 7.
the three rami of the *lateral cerebral sulcus* (Sylvius). It corresponds on the surface to a point known as the *pterion* which is situated $1\frac{1}{4}$ inches behind the zygomatic process of the frontal bone, and $1\frac{1}{2}$ inches above the upper border of the zygomatic process of the temporal bone. The main posterior ramus of the
Fig. i, 10,
11.
sulcus passes backwards and upwards from the Sylvian point to a second point situated $\frac{3}{4}$ inch below the most prominent part of the parietal bone (parietal prominence).

The anterior ascending ramus is directed upwards for
Fig. i, 8, 9.
about $\frac{3}{4}$ inch, whilst the anterior horizontal ramus passes forwards for about the same distance.

The pterion corresponds also to the anterior pole of the *insula* and to the *middle cerebral artery*, as that vessel lies deeply embedded in the anterior part of the lateral cerebral sulcus.

To mark out the *parieto-occipital* sulcus and the *superior temporal sulcus*, it is necessary to find two bony points—the
Fig. i, 12-
15.
marginal tubercle of the zygomatic bone and the lambda. A line uniting these two points corresponds in its posterior part to the parieto-occipital sulcus, and in its middle third to the superior temporal sulcus.

The *central sulcus (fissure of Rolando).*—Take a point

Fig. i, 4. $\frac{1}{2}$ inch behind the centre of a line drawn across the vertex of the skull from the nasion to the inion, and from this point draw a line downwards and forwards for $3\frac{1}{2}$ to 4 inches, at an angle of $67\frac{1}{2}°$ (three-quarters of a right-angle) to the median antero-posterior line. From a more practical point of view, it suffices to draw a line (for the required distance) from the above point towards the centre of the zygomatic process. In front of this sulcus is the precentral gyrus—an area better known as the *Rolandic* or *motor area*. The main centres here situated correspond, from above downwards, to the movements of the *lower limb*, *upper limb* and *face* of the opposite side of the body. Immediately posterior to the central sulcus lies the postcentral gyrus, the somaesthetic area, with a corresponding arrangement of cortical areas.

The superior temporal line cuts across the central sulcus Fig. i, 5. at the junction of its lower and middle thirds. It may be regarded as the line of demarcation between the upper extremity area above and the face area below.

On the left side of the head, that part of the brain which is included in the obtuse angle between the anterior hori- Fig. i. zontal and the posterior rami of the lateral cerebral sulcus is known as *Broca's area* (the motor speech centre).

The *middle meningeal artery*, a branch of the maxillary artery, enters the skull through the foramen spinosum, and divides, after a short and variable course across the middle fossa of the skull, into two main trunks. The seat Fig. ii, 3. of bifurcation usually corresponds to a point just above the centre of the zygoma.

The anterior branch is not only the larger of the two but it is also more liable to injury, since it is protected in

Fig. ii, 4. the temporal region by a comparatively thin osseous covering.

Fig. ii, 5, 5, 5. The danger zone in the course of this branch may be mapped out by taking three points :

(1) 1 inch behind the zygomatic process of the frontal bone and the same distance above the corresponding process of the temporal bone.

(2) 1½ inches behind and above the same processes.

(3) 2 inches behind and above the same processes—the *anterior meningeal point.*

A line uniting these three points represents the more vulnerable part of the artery.

The anterior division of the vessel will be exposed by trephining over any of these three points, but it is advisable to select the highest—the anterior meningeal point—as by such means the posterior border of the great wing of the sphenoid is avoided ; and, as an additional reason, it should be added that, in the position of points 1 and 2, the artery frequently runs in an osseous canal. After trephining over the upper point, the bone can be chipped away in a downward and forward direction, if such an exposure of the artery is deemed necessary.

Fig. ii, 6. The *posterior branch of the artery* passes almost horizontally backwards, parallel to the zygomatic process of the temporal bone and to the supra-mastoid crest, and it can be exposed by trephining over a

Fig. ii, 7. point where a vertical line drawn upwards from the posterior border of the mastoid process cuts another line drawn backwards from the supra-orbital margin parallel to Reid's base-line—the *posterior meningeal point.*

The *lateral ventricles.*—The inferior cornu of the lateral ventricle may be tapped by trephining immediately above and behind the posterior meningeal point. The

Fig. ii, 8. needle should be directed towards the summit of the opposite ear, the ventricle being reached within 2 inches from the surface (Keen).

The *basic fossæ.*—" There is no external sign to indicate the situation of the fossæ of the skull. In general, however, it may be said that the anterior fossa extends as far back as the anterior end of the zygoma ; that the middle fossa lies between this and the mastoid process, and the posterior includes all the base behind the process " (Eisendrath).

The *tympanic antrum* may be exposed by trephining in

Fig. ii, 12a. *Macewen's suprameatal triangle,* a space which
Fig. ii, 12. is bounded above by the backward continuation of the posterior root of the zygoma (the supramastoid crest), behind by a vertical line drawn upwards from the posterior border of the external auditory meatus, and below and in front by the *suprameatal spine,* a prominent bony process which assists in the formation of the posterior superior quadrant of the external auditory meatus. In this triangle there is usually a well-marked depression—the *suprameatal fossa.* The supramastoid crest not only indicates the uppermost possible limit of the tympanic antrum, but, as has already been stated, it corresponds also to the level of the base of brain in this situation. The crest, therefore, represents the level

Fig. ii, 13. of the *tegmen tympani,* and, in mastoid explorations, the field of operation must be confined to an area below this crest. In the adult the antrum usually lies at a depth of $\frac{1}{2}$ to $\frac{3}{4}$ inch from the surface. In the child it is much nearer the surface.

The *transverse venous sinus* lies posterior and nearer to

Fig. ii, 9. the surface, whilst the *facial nerve* pursues its
Fig. ii, 12b. course in front and on a deeper plane.

The *parotid gland* occupies the space which is bounded

Fig. iii, 2.
above by the zygomatic arch, behind by the auricle and the mastoid process, and below by a line drawn from the angle of the jaw to the apex of the mastoid process. In front, the gland extends a variable distance over the anterior surface of the *masseter* muscle. This muscle passes downwards and backwards from the lower border of the zygomatic arch to be attached to the outer surface of the descending ramus and angle of the lower jaw. When the teeth are clenched, the anterior border of the muscle is easily defined, a well-marked line of demarcation being so formed between the masseter muscle behind and the buccinator in front.

Parotid (Stenson's) duct, the duct of the parotid gland,

Fig. iii, 3.
corresponds to the middle third of a line drawn from the lower border of the tragus of the ear to a point situated half-way between the ala of the nose and the red line of the upper lip. At the anterior border of the masseter muscle the duct dips inwards, through the buccinator muscle, to open on the buccal mucous membrane, opposite the second molar tooth of the upper jaw.

The *transverse facial artery*, a branch of the superficial

Fig. iii, 4.
temporal, runs forwards parallel to and immediately below the zygoma, lying above the level of the parotid duct.

The *facial nerve*, after emerging from the stylo-mastoid

Fig. iii, 5.
foramen, curls round the neck of the mandible, and traverses the substance of the parotid gland, in which part of its course it divides into numerous branches. The general transparotid course of the nerve and the direction of its buccal branch may be indicated by a line drawn forwards parallel to, and below the parotid duct from the lobule of the ear.

The *mandibular nerve* may be represented by a line drawn from the midpoint of the zygoma downwards towards the mandibular foramen—a point midway between the anterior and posterior margins of the ramus of the lower jaw, just below the level of the alveolar border, then forwards to the mental foramen (see below).

The *borders of the bony orbit.*—The following bones assist in the formation of the orbital margin :

Superior, the frontal bone.

Laterally, the zygomatic process of the frontal bone and the corresponding process of the zygomatic bone.

Inferior, the zygomatic bone and the maxilla.

Medially, the frontal process of the maxilla and the internal angular frontal process.

The *medial palpebral ligament (tendo oculi) and naso-lacrimal duct.*—By alternate forcible closure and opening of the lids, the medial palpebral ligament can be felt passing to its insertion into the frontal process of the maxilla. Immediately below the tendon, at the junction of the medial and inferior walls of the orbital cavity, is the depression for the lacrimal sac, which sac narrows below into the *nasolacrimal duct.* The duct passes from the inner canthus in a downward, backward and slightly outward direction to open into the anterior part of the inferior meatus of the nose under cover of the inferior concha. It is about ½ inch long.

Fig. ii, 17.

Fig. ii, 18.

The *supra-orbital, infra-orbital, and mental foramina.*— At the junction of the inner and middle thirds of the supra-orbital margin, the supra-orbital notch or foramen may be felt, and a line drawn downwards from this foramen through the interval between the two lower bicuspid teeth will pass through both infra-orbital and mental foramina. The former foramen lies

Fig. v, 1, 2, 3.

$\frac{1}{4}$ to $\frac{1}{2}$ inch below the orbital margin, whilst the latter (in the adult) lies midway between the alveolar and inferior borders of the lower jaw.

The *frontal sinuses* are very variable in extent and seldom symmetrical. They occupy the space between the inner and outer tables of the frontal bone, above the base of the nose and above the inner half of the supra-orbital margin. The sinus communicates with the nasal cavity by means of a narrow channel, the *fronto-nasal duct* which opens into the middle meatus of the nose under cover of the middle concha, on a level with the inner margin of the palpebral fissure.

The *maxillary sinus* (*antrum of Highmore*) usually occupies the greater part of the interior of the maxilla, and opens into the *hiatus semilunaris*—a depression which lies under cover of the middle concha. The opening is, however, situated at so high a level that pus only escapes into the nose when the antrum is practically full. Two teeth are closely related to the antrum, namely, the second bicuspid and the first molar, the antrum usually extending downwards in the interval between the two labial and single palatal fangs of the latter tooth.

The *sphenoidal sinus* occupies the greater part of the body of the sphenoid, and opens into the spheno-ethmoidal recess, a space lying above and behind the superior concha.

The sinuses of the nose and their efferent channels :

The sphenoidal sinus → spheno-ethmoidal recess.

The posterior ethmoidal sinus → superior meatus.

The anterior ethmoidal sinus ⎫
The middle ethmoidal sinus ⎪
⎬ → middle meatus.
The frontal sinus ⎪
The maxillary sinus ⎭

The nasolacrimal duct → inferior meatus.

The *mouth.*—In the median line hangs the *uvula.* The soft palate, traced in the outward direction, is seen to diverge into the two *pillars of the fauces*—anterior pillar (palatoglossus) and posterior pillar (palatopharyngeus)—enclosing a triangular recess, at the base of which the *tonsil* is situated.

The dorsum of the tongue is divided into an anterior two-thirds and a posterior third by a V-shaped furrow, the *sulcus terminalis,* the limbs of which pass obliquely forwards from the foramen cæcum. The papillæ of the tongue—*vallate* (8–12 in number, immediately anterior to the sulcus terminalis), *fungiform, filiform* and *simplex*—are supplied by the lingual branch of the mandibular nerve (ordinary sensibility), chorda tympani (special taste for anterior two-thirds) and by branches from the glossopharyngeal to the vallate papillæ (taste).

When the tip of the tongue is turned up, the *frenulum* is seen, passing in the middle line from tip to base when it meets two lateral irregular folds which correspond to the underlying ducts of the submandibular gland (*Wharton's ducts*). In close proximity to the junction of these mucous folds two papillæ are seen, one on either side of the middle line—the openings of the ducts.

Running lateral to the frenum, but diverging outwards, the two *lingual veins* are seen, and, still more lateral, two fringed mucous folds, the plica fimbriata. On everting the cheek, the orifice of the parotid duct will be observed, opening opposite the second upper molar tooth.

The *teeth :* (1) *Deciduous teeth.*—When the child is between 2 and 3 years old, all deciduous teeth, ten in each jaw, should be present. Though subject to considerable variation they appear at about the following dates :

Lower Central incisors   .   6th month.

Upper incisors .   .   .   9th   ,,

Lower lateral incisors and } 15th   ,,
    1st molars   .   .   . }

Canines .   .   .   .   18th   ,,

2nd molars   .   .   .   24th   ,,

(2) *Permanent teeth.*—When complete, there are sixteen in each jaw. They appear at or about the following dates:

1st molars   .   .   .   6th year.

Central incisors   .   .   7th   ,,

Lateral incisors   .   .   8th   ,,

1st premolars   .   .   9th   ,,

2nd premolars   .   .   10th   ,,

Canines   .   .   .   11th   ,,

2nd molars   .   .   .   12th   ,,

3rd molars   .   .   . From 17th to 25th year.

The Triangles of the Neck.

The lateral aspect of the neck is divided by the sterno-mastoid muscle into two triangles—anterior and posterior.

The *anterior triangle* is bounded in front by the middle line of the neck, behind by the anterior border of the sternomastoid muscle, and above by the lower border of the ramus of the mandible.

Fig. iv.

The space so marked out is divided into three smaller triangles by the digastric muscle and by the anterior belly of the omohyoid :

Fig. iv, 5. (1) The *digastric* triangle, above the digastric muscle, containing the submandibular gland.

Fig. iv, 11. (2) The *muscular* triangle, anterior to the omohyoid muscle, bounded by the anterior belly of the omohyoid, the anterior border of the sterno-mastoid, and by the median vertical line.

2

(3) The *carotid* triangle, bounded above by the posterior belly of the digastric, behind by the anterior border of the sternomastoid muscle, and in front by the anterior belly of the omohyoid. In this triangle the common carotid bifurcates, and the external carotid gives off most of its branches.

Fig. iv, 10.

The *posterior* triangle is bounded in front by the posterior border of the sternomastoid, behind by the anterior border of the trapezius, and below by the middle third or fourth of the clavicle. The triangle is subdivided by the posterior belly of the omohyoid, which cuts off the small *supraclavicular* triangle below from the more extensive *occipital* triangle above.

Fig. iv.

The Vessels and Nerves.

The *carotid arteries* correspond in direction to a line from the sternoclavicular joint to the hollow between the angle of the mandible and the mastoid process. The *common carotid* usually bifurcates at the level of the upper border of the thyroid cartilage (fourth cervical vertebra), the external carotid subsequently lying superficial to and slightly to the inner side of the internal carotid. The *omohyoid* muscle (upper belly) crosses the common carotid at the level of the cricoid cartilage, and in this situation the artery may be compressed against the prominent anterior tubercle of the transverse process of the sixth cervical vertebra (Chassaignac's tubercle).

Fig. iii, 6.

Fig. iii, 7, 8.

The *superior thyroid* artery arises from the external carotid in the carotid triangle, immediately above the level of the upper border of the thyroid carti-lage, and, turning downwards under cover of the anterior belly of the omohyoid muscle, is directed

Fig. iii, 11.

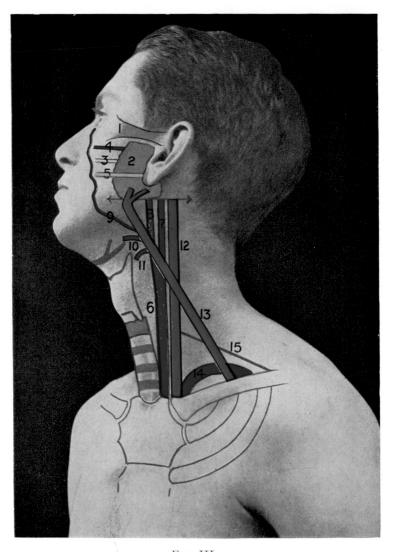

FIG. III.

1. Zygoma.
2. Parotid gland.
3. Parotid duct (Stenson).
4. Transverse facial artery.
5. Facial nerve (buccal branch).
6. Common carotid triangle.
7. Internal carotid artery.
8. External carotid artery.
9. Facial artery.
10. Lingual artery.
11. Superior thyroid artery.
12. Internal jugular vein.
13. External jugular vein.
14. Subclavian artery.
15. Upper limit of brachial plexus.

To face Fig. IV, pp. 14, 15.

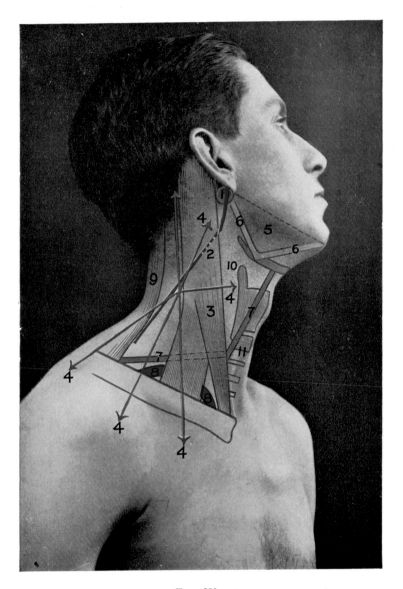

FIG. IV.

1. Transverse process of the atlas.
2. The accessory nerve (spinal accessory).
3. Sternomastoid muscle.
4, 4. Superficial cervical plexus.
5. Digastric triangle.
6, 6. Anterior and posterior bellies of the digastric muscle.
7, 7. Anterior and posterior bellies of the omohyoid muscle.
8, 8. Supraclavicular triangle.
9. Posterior triangle.
10. Carotid triangle.
11. Muscular triangle.

To face Fig. III, pp. 14, 15.

towards the apex of the lateral lobe of the thyroid gland.

The *lingual artery* arises midway between the level of the upper border of the thyroid cartilage and the great **Fig. iii, 10.** cornu of the hyoid bone, and enters the digastric triangle by passing deep to the digastric muscle. The artery so gains the upper border of the hyoid bone, and runs inwards for a short distance parallel to that bone under cover of the hyoglossus muscle.

The *facial artery* arises opposite the great cornu of the hyoid bone, and enters the digastric triangle by **Fig. iii, 9.** passing deep to the tendon of the digastric. In this triangle the artery lies deeply embedded in the substance of the submandibular salivary gland, and then enters on its facial course by curling round the inferior border of the mandible immediately anterior to the masseter muscle, about $1\frac{1}{2}$ inches in front of the angle of the mandible. The vessel then passes upwards towards the inner canthus of the eye, there terminating as the " angular artery."

The *occipital artery* arises from the posterior part of the external carotid artery in the upper part of the carotid triangle, and passes upwards and backwards, under cover of the posterior belly of the digastric muscle, towards the interval between the mastoid process and the transverse process of the atlas. At the apex of the posterior triangle the artery is joined by the greater occipital nerve (posterior primary ramus of the second cervical nerve), the two structures then passing upwards on to the vault of the skull.

The *posterior auricular artery* arises from the external carotid, immediately above the posterior belly of the digastric muscle, and passes backwards parallel to the upper border of that muscle, under cover of the lower part of the parotid gland, to the depression between the cartilage of the concha of the ear and the mastoid process. Here the artery is joined by the posterior auricular nerve —a branch of the facial.

The *superficial temporal artery* arises in the substance of the parotid gland as one of the two terminal branches of the external carotid. It crosses the base of the zygomatic process of the temporal bone, immediately in front of the tragus of the ear, and is accompanied by the auriculo-temporal nerve—a sensory branch of the third division of the fifth cranial nerve.

The *subclavian artery* (cervical course) is represented by **Fig. iii, 14. Fig. iv, 8.** a curved line from the sternoclavicular joint to the mid-point of the clavicle, the convexity of the line extending upwards into the supra-clavicular fossa about ¾ to 1 inch above the clavicle. In marking out this vessel, the shoulders should be well depressed.

The artery passes behind the *scalenus anterior* muscle the second part of the artery being covered by that muscle. The outer border of the scalene muscle usually corresponds to the outer border of the sternomastoid muscle, and consequently the third part of the subclavian artery is **Fig. iv, 8.** represented by that part of the curve which lies between the outer border of the sterno-mastoid muscle and the mid-point of the clavicle.

The subclavian artery ends anatomically at the outer border of the first rib.

The *external jugular vein* is formed just behind the angle of the mandible by the junction of the posterior division of the posterior facial vein with the posterior auricular vein.

The vessel so formed passes downwards and backwards,
Fig. iii, 13. superficial to the sternomastoid muscle, but deep to the platysma, towards the middle of the clavicle, where it pierces the deep fascia to join the subclavian vein. It is represented by a line drawn from the angle of the mandible to the middle of the clavicle.

The *internal jugular vein* runs parallel and external to Fig. iii, 12. the internal and common carotid arteries, and therefore presents a similar surface marking to that already given for those vessels.

The *vagus nerve* passes downwards in the carotid sheath, behind and between the carotid arteries and the internal jugular vein.

The *cervical sympathetic trunk* also lies in the line of the carotid arteries, being placed behind the carotid sheath. The *superior cervical ganglion* is situated in front of the transverse processes of the second and third cervical vertebræ ; the *middle ganglion* overlies the corresponding process of the sixth vertebra ; whilst the *inferior ganglion*, which is frequently fused with the first thoracic, lies behind the first part of the subclavian artery, between the transverse process of the seventh cervical vertebra and the neck of the first rib.

The *phrenic nerve* is formed below the level of the hyoid bone by branches from the anterior primary rami of the third, fourth and fifth cervical nerves, and passes downwards and slightly inwards obliquely across the front of the scalenus anterior, towards the sternal end of the clavicle. At the level of the cricoid cartilage the nerve lies midway between the anterior and posterior borders of the sternomastoid muscle.

The *accessory nerve* crosses the transverse process of the atlas—a bony prominence to be felt immediately below and in front of the apex of the mastoid process. The nerve enters the substance of the sternomastoid at the junction of the upper and second quarters along Fig. iv, 2. the anterior border of the muscle, emerging from the posterior border of the muscle at the junction of the upper and middle thirds. The point of emergence is, however, subject to some variation, and the nerve may enter the posterior triangle of the neck at a somewhat lower level, pursuing subsequently a downward and backward course towards the anterior border of the trapezius muscle, beneath which muscle it sinks.*

The *superficial cervical plexus.*—Take a point midway Fig.iv, 4. along the posterior border of the sternomastoid muscle, and from this point draw three lines:

1. Upwards towards the lobe of the ear = the great auricular nerve (2 and 3 C.).

2. Upwards along the posterior border of the sterno-mastoid muscle = lesser occipital nerve (2 C.).

3. Forwards towards the middle line of the neck = the anterior cutaneous nerve (2 and 3 C.).

These three lines produced downwards represent the direction of the descending branches of the plexus. Thus, the great auricular produced = the intermediate supra-clavicular nerve, the anterior cutaneous = the lateral supraclavicular nerve, and the lesser occipital = the medial supraclavicular nerve. These three descending branches are derived from the 3rd and 4th cervical nerves.

* Another surface-marking for the *spinal accessory nerve.*— Draw a line from a point midway between the tip of the mastoid process and the angle of the mandible to the middle of the posterior border of the sternomastoid muscle, and thence across the posterior triangle to the anterior border of trapezius.

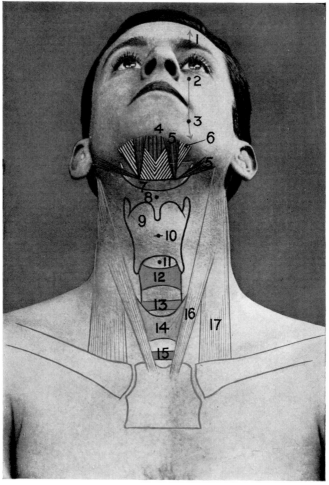

FIG. V.

1. Supraorbital foramen.
2. Infraorbital foramen.
3. Mental foramen.
4. Genio-hyoid muscle.
5, 5. Anterior and posterior bellies of the digastric muscle.
6. Mylohyoid muscle.
7. Hyoid bone.
8. Thyrohyoid membrane, and epiglottis.
9. Thyroid cartilage.
10. Rima glottidis.
11. Cricothyroid ligament and cricovocal membrane.
12. Cricoid cartilage.
13. First ring of trachea.
14. Isthmus of the thyroid gland.
15. Tracheal ring.
16. Sternal head of sterno-mastoid muscle.
17. Clavicular head of sterno-mastoid.

To face p. 19.

The *brachial plexus*.—The upper limit of the nerve-
trunks which form this plexus is represented
by a line drawn from the mid-point between
the anterior and posterior borders of the sternomastoid
muscle at the level of the cricoid cartilage to a second
point situated just external to the mid-point of the
clavicle. The lowest cord lies behind the third part of
the subclavian artery.

Fig. iii, 15.

The *rima glottidis*, bounded laterally by the true
vocal cords, lies opposite the mid-point along
the anterior border of the thyroid cartilage.

Fig. v, 10.

The *epiglottis*, though fixed below to the thyroid angle
immediately above the point of attachment of
the true vocal cords, extends upwards to above
the level of the body of the hyoid bone.

Fig. v, 8.

A suicidal cut-throat frequently involves the thyrohyoid membrane, and the epiglottis may be severed from
its thyroid attachment.

The *isthmus of the thyroid gland* crosses the trachea
about $\frac{1}{2}$ to $\frac{3}{4}$ inch below the cricoid cartilage.
The *lateral lobes* extend upwards to the middle
of the thyroid cartilage, downwards nearly to the clavicle,
and outwards to be overlapped by the sternomastoid
muscle.

Fig. v, 14.

Fig. v. *The structures in the middle line of the neck :*

(1) Passing down from the mandible to the body of
the hyoid bone, the two geniohyoid muscles lie each side
of the middle line. (2) The body of the hyoid bone.
(3) The thyrohyoid membrane. (4) The thyroid cartilage. (5) The cricothyroid ligament and cricovocal membrane. (6) The cricoid cartilage. (7) The first ring of
the trachea. (8) The isthmus of the thyroid gland. (9)
The trachea. (10) The suprasternal notch.

CHAPTER II

THE UPPER LIMB

In this chapter, and in that on the lower extremity, the reader's attention is directed mainly to those bony prominences, and muscular or tendinous elevations, which lie in the region of the joints, since these form the more important landmarks which aid in the representation of the arteries, nerves, etc., of the limbs. The muscular masses, which complete the symmetry of the arm or leg between the joints, are only mentioned where necessary, a fair general knowledge of the anatomical structure of the body being assumed.

The *Shoulder region.*The acromion, the spine of the scapula and the clavicle, being subcutaneous throughout their whole length, can readily be palpated from end to end. The clavicle should be examined first, from its blunted sternal extremity to the acromio-clavicular joint. The inner third of the shaft is rounded and presents a marked forward convexity, whilst the outer third of the bone is flattened from before backwards and shows a concave anterior border. At the outer end of the bone a slight elevation may be felt on the superior surface, and immediately external to this is the acromio-clavicular joint, the long axis of which lies in the antero-posterior direction.

20

The acromial spine is narrow at about its centre, broadening out towards the vertebral border of the scapula and forming there a smooth triangular surface, over which glides the tendinous part of the trapezius. Laterally, the spine terminates in the upward curved Fig. xiii, acromial process, at the anterior border of 1. which an oval facet is situated for articulation with the clavicle. The supra- and infraspinatus muscles fill up the depressions or fossæ which lie above and below the spine of the acromion.

The clavicle is also bounded above and below by depressions, little evident in fat subjects, but most marked when, as the result of pathological or physiological conditions, fat is feebly represented. The supraclavicular or subclavian triangle is dealt with in the first chapter. The *infraclavicular space* is bounded above by the clavicle, below by the clavicular head of the pectoralis major muscle, medially by the costal cartilage of the first rib, and laterally by the anterior border of the deltoid muscle. The floor is formed by the subclavius muscle and the clavi-pectoral fascia. In the outer part of the space the coracoid process may be felt, lying under cover of the anterior border of the deltoid muscle, 1 inch below the Fig. xiii. junction of the outer and middle thirds of the clavicle. The bulky deltoid muscle, arising from the clavicle, and from the acromion and the spine of the scapula, is, so to speak, pushed outwards by the underlying head and greater tuberosity of the humerus, so producing the normal rounded appearance of the shoulder. This outward displacement of the muscle is taken advantage of by Hamilton in the diagnosis of a dislocation of the shoulder-joint, as, after such an injury, the humerus is drawn inwards by the pectoralis major, latissimus dorsi

and other muscles to such a degree that a ruler placed
along the outer side of the arm will be in contact with
the acromion and the lateral epicondyle of the humerus at
one and the same time.   In the normal condition this is
not possible.

To measure the *length of the humerus*, the tape-measure
Fig. xiii,   should be carried from the lower margin of
1–2.   the acromion to the lateral epicondyle of the
humerus.

Between the greater and lesser tuberosities of the
humerus is the *bicipital groove*, in which runs the long
tendon of the biceps muscle.   The groove may be
represented by a line, about 2 inches long, which runs
downwards from the tip of the acromion, parallel to the
long axis of the humerus.

The *upper epiphysis* of the humerus includes the head
and both tuberosities, and the epiphysial line runs transversely, at right angles to the long axis of the humerus, at
the lower border of the great tuberosity.

The *axilla*.—To examine this space, the elbow should
be supported, and the patient instructed to relax all
muscles.   The anterior wall is formed by the major and
minor pectoral muscles, and by the clavi-pectoral fascia.
The pectoralis major alone forms the anterior fold of the
Fig. vi, 3.   axilla, and does not extend as far downwards as the posterior fold, whilst its rounded
appearance results from the twisting of the fibres of the
muscle previous to insertion into the outer bicipital
ridge.   The posterior wall is formed by the latissimus dorsi,
teres major and subscapularis muscles.   The rounding of
the posterior fold of the axilla is due to the latissimus
dorsi, which curls round the teres major muscle from behind forwards in order to reach its insertion into the floor

THE FRONT OF THE ARM AND FOREARM

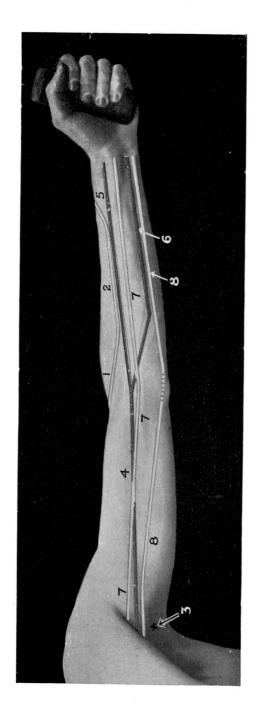

Fig. VI.

1. ⎫
2. ⎭ The radial nerve.

3. The axilla.
4. Brachial artery.

5. Radial artery.
6. Ulnar artery.

7, 7. Median nerve.
8, 8. Ulnar nerve.

To face p. 22.

THE ELBOW AND BACK REGION

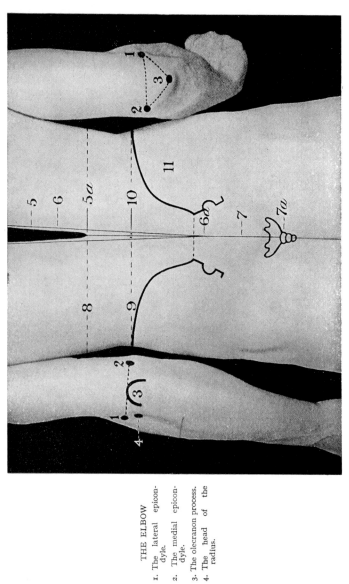

FIG. VII.

THE BACK.

THE ELBOW

1. The lateral epicondyle.
2. The medial epicondyle.
3. The olecranon process.
4. The head of the radius.

5. The spinal cord.
5a. The termination of the cord at the level of the transpyloric plane (1st lumbar vertebra).
The spinal dural sheath.

6a. The termination of the subarachnoid space at the level of the 3rd sacral vertebra, just below a line drawn transversely between the two posterior superior iliac spines.

7. The filum terminale.
7a. The termination of the filum near the tip or the coccyx.
8. The transpyloric plane.

9. The transtubercular plane (highest point of iliac crests).
10. The site for lumbar puncture.
11. The iliac crests.   *To face p. 23.*

of the bicipital groove. The narrow outer boundary of the axilla corresponds to the upper part of the shaft and to the head of the humerus, and in this situation, in a well-developed arm, two prominent longitudinal folds are seen, the anterior of which corresponds to the coraco-brachialis and biceps (short head) muscles, whilst the more posterior fold results from the projection of the neuro-vascular bundle. The head of the humerus and of the scapula can be felt at the upper and posterior part of the axilla, the second rib on the inner side, and the cora-coid process in front. The head of the humerus looks in the same direction as the medial epicondyle of the humerus. The inner wall of the axilla is formed by the upper part of the lateral wall of the thorax, which is here clothed by the serrations of the serratus anterior muscle.

The *axillary lymphatic glands* are arranged in three main groups, all converging towards the apex of the axilla :

(*a*) The *pectoral* set, running upwards and outwards under cover of the outer border of the pectoral muscles, and draining the anterior and lateral aspects of the chest-wall and the abdomen above the level of the umbilicus.

(*b*) The *subscapular* set, running upwards along the axillary border of the subscapularis muscle, and draining the lateral and posterior aspect of the chest above the level of the umbilicus.

(*c*) The *brachial and axillary* set, running upwards in the line of the axillary vessels, and draining the whole of the upper limb.

The *Elbow region.*—When the forearm is extended, a line joining the medial and lateral epicondyles

Fig. vii, 1–3. of the humerus cuts across the tip of the olecranon process, which bony prominence lies well to the medial side of the mid-point of the intercondyloid line.

When the forearm is flexed, the olecranon moves downwards, and by uniting the three bony points

Fig. vii, 4.

a triangle is formed. Immediately below the
lateral epicondyle the head of the radius is felt "lying
in the valley behind the brachioradialis" (Holden).
The humero-radial articulation is transverse, but the
humero-ulnar articulation slopes obliquely downwards
and inwards, and consequently, whilst the lateral epicondyle is about ¾ inch above the humero-radial joint,
the medial epicondyle lies rather more than 1 inch above
the line of the humero-ulnar articulation.

The junction of the *diaphysis* and *lower epiphysis* of the
humerus corresponds to a transverse line drawn across
the humerus immediately above the tips of the epicondyles. The bony points on the outer side of the joint are
generally obscured in those cases where there is considerable effusion into the elbow-joint, the synovial membrane
bulging outwards below the lateral epicondyle of the
humerus and between that process and the olecranon
process. Under similar conditions there is also an outward projection of the synovial membrane between the
olecranon and the medial epicondyle of the humerus,
obscuring the deep depression that normally exists in that
situation—a depression at the base of which the ulnar
nerve can be rolled beneath the finger.

In front of the elbow is the *cubital fossa*, a triangular
space, the base of which corresponds to a line

Fig. viii, 1, 1.

drawn across the front of the elbow between
the two humeral epicondyles, whilst the inner and outer

Fig. viii, 4, 5.

boundaries are formed respectively by the pronator teres and brachioradialis muscles. This

Fig. viii, 2.

triangular space is vertically subdivided by the
biceps tendon, on either side of which a depres-

THE ELBOW REGION

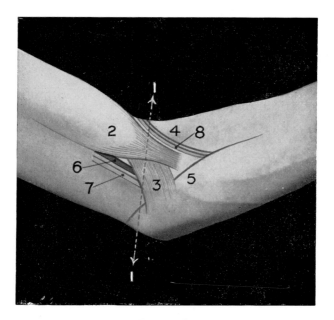

Fig. VIII.

1. The inter-condyloid line.
2. Biceps muscle.
3. Bicipital aponeurosis.
4. Brachioradialis.
5. Pronator radii teres.
6. Brachial artery.
7. Median nerve.
8. Radial nerve.

To face p. 24.

THE VEINS OF THE ARM AND FOREARM

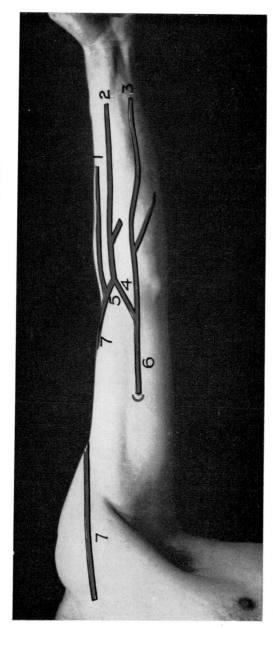

Fig. IX.

1. Radial veins.   3. Ulnar veins.   5. Median cephalic vein   7. Cephalic vein.
2. Median veins.   4. Median basilic vein.   6. Basilic vein.

To follow Fig. VIII.

sion exists—the inner and outer *bicipital sulci*. In the outer

Fig. viii, 8.

sulcus the radial nerve gives origin to its posterior interosseous branch and is then continued as a pure sensory nerve. The median nerve and the brachial

Fig. viii, 6, 7.

artery lie in the inner sulcus, the artery intermediate between the tendon and the nerve. The artery and nerve are, however, obscured in the lower

Fig. viii, 3.

part of the inner sulcus by the overlaying *bicipital aponeurosis*, which can be traced inwards to the pronator region, whilst its upper free margin presents a well-marked crescentic edge which looks upwards and inwards. This aponeurosis becomes well defined on forcible flexion of the elbow.

The *superficial veins* in front of the bend of the elbow

Fig. ix.

are arranged in the form of a letter M, the radial, median and ulnar group of veins being received from below, whilst the two main efferent vessels,

Fig. ix, 6.

the cephalic and the basilic, carry the blood upwards. The *basilic vein* passes upwards in the superficial fascia, along the inner side of the arm, and pierces the deep fascia about half-way between the axilla and the medial epicondyle, and at the foramen so produced in the deep fascia the medial antebrachial cutaneous nerve emerges to become superficial. The *epitrochlear gland* lies in close connection with the median basilic or basilic veins above and in front of the internal condyle.

The *cephalic vein* can be traced upwards along the outer

Fig. ix, 7.

side of the arm as far as the groove between the deltoid and pectoralis major muscles. In the interval between these two muscles the vein lies

Fig. ix, 7.

embedded, and eventually pierces the clavipectoral fascia in the infraclavicular region to open into the axillary vein.

THE REGION OF THE WRIST AND HAND

Two tendons only are conspicuous at the front of the wrist—the palmaris longus in the middle line and the flexor carpi radialis to the outer side of the palmaris longus. The flexor carpi ulnaris can, however, be distinguished by palpation along the ulnar border of the forearm, and can be traced downwards to its insertion into the pisiform bone. Between the palmaris longus and the flexor carpi ulnaris the main mass of the flexor digitorum sublimis lies. Two transverse creases are seen in this situation, the upper of which corresponds roughly to the level of the radiocarpal joint, while the lower represents almost exactly the upper limit of the flexor retinaculum (transverse carpal ligament).

Just lateral to where the flexor carpi radialis tendon cuts across the two transverse creases there is a depression, in the floor of which the lower end of the radius and the tubercle of the scaphoid bone may be felt. The radial artery crosses this space in a downward and outward direction. The trapezium lies at the lower limit of the depression, immediately below and external to the scaphoid tuberosity. The prominent pisiform bone can be distinguished by tracing downwards the tendon of the flexor carpi ulnaris muscle, and posterior to this bone both triquetral and hamate bones are situated. A finger's breadth below and lateral to the pisiform bone deep palpation will verify the position of the hook of the hamate bone.

The *flexor retinaculum* is attached to four bony points, two on the radial side, the scaphoid tubercle and the ridge on the trapezium, and

Fig. x, 2, 3.

Fig. x, 5, 6.

Fig. x, 7.

Fig. x, 1.

Fig. x, 5, 6.

Fig. xi, 5.

Fig. xi, 1.

FIG. X.

1. Radial artery.
2. Flexor carpi radialis.
3. Palmaris longus.
4. Ulnar artery.
5. Flexor carpi ulnaris.
6. The pisiform bone.
7. The two transverse creases in front of the joint.
8. The superficial branch of the ulnar artery, forming with the superficial palmar branch of the radial artery, the superficial palmar arch.
9, 9. The digital branches of the superficial palmar arch.
10. The deep branch of the ulnar, forming the deep palmar arch, passing between the two heads of the first dorsal interosseous muscle, to join the radial.

THE PALM OF THE HAND

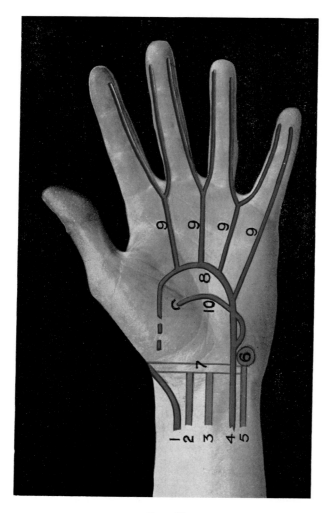

Fig. X.

To face p. 26.

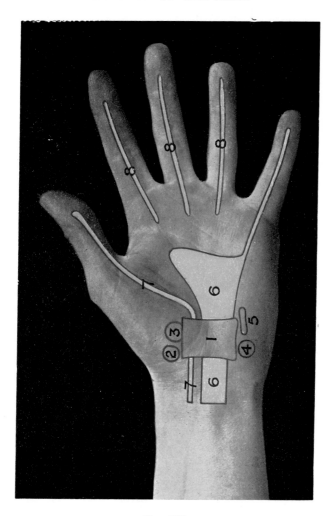

Fig. XI.

1. The flexor retinaculum.
2. Scaphoid tubercle.
3. Ridge of trapezium.
4. Pisiform bone.
5. Hook of hamate.
6. Common flexor synovial sheath.
7. Flexor pollicis longus sheath.
8, 8. Distal flexor sheaths.

To follow Fig. X.

two on the ulnar side, the pisiform and the hook of the hamate. The upper limit of the ligament corresponds to the lower of the two transverse creases in front of the wrist, whilst the inferior limit of the ligament lies about ¾ inch below.

The *flexor synovial sheaths.*—The flexor pollicis longus,

Fig. xi.   the flexor digitorum sublimis and profundus all pass beneath the flexor retinaculum. In this situation the flexor sublimis consists of four tendons, of which the medius and annularis lie superficial to the tendons which pass to the index and little fingers. The profundus consists of two parts only, the tendon to the index-finger being alone differentiated off from the main mass. Beneath the ligament these tendons are surrounded by two synovial sheaths, one for the flexor pollicis longus and one for the remaining tendons plus the median nerve. These sheaths extend upwards about 1 inch above the upper limit of the ligament, and therefore the same distance above the lower transverse

Fig. xi,   crease in front of the wrist. The flexor pollicis
6, 6.   longus sheath is continued downwards to the insertion of the tendon into the distal phalanx of the thumb. The main sheath broadens out below the ligament, and though generally continued onwards to the end of the

Fig. xi.   little finger, the major portion terminates at the level of the upper transverse crease of the palm. The flexor tendons to the index, middle and ring fingers also possess more distally distinct synovial sheaths, which extend from the terminal phalanges of the fingers upwards to the necks of the metacarpal bones, a level corresponding roughly to the lower transverse crease of the palm.

A distance of ½ inch separates the main synovial sheath above from the more distal segments below.

3

On the lateral side of the wrist the most marked feature is the "anatomical snuff-box"—a space bounded on the radial side by the tendons of the abductor pollicis longus and extensor pollicis brevis muscles, and on the ulnar side by the tendon of the extensor pollicis longus.

In the floor of the space the styloid process of the radius is felt, this prominence lying fully $\frac{1}{2}$ inch below the level of the corresponding process of the ulna, and also on a slightly more anterior plane. Immediately below the radial styloid process the scaphoid bone lies, most prominent when the hand is well adducted. Below this, again, the trapezium and the bases of the first and second metacarpals are to be felt.

On the dorsum of the hand there is a well-marked elevation, most noticeable when the wrist is fully flexed, due to the projection of the bases of the second and third metacarpal bones, the styloid process of the latter bone being especially prominent.

Immediately above this elevation there is a depression where the tendons of the extensor carpi radialis longus and brevis are felt as they pass to their insertion into the bases of the second and third metacarpal bones.

Near the middle of the posterior aspect of the lower end of the radius a tubercle can generally be distinguished—*the dorsal tubercle (Lister)*—separating the extensor pollicis longus on the medial side from the tendon of the extensor carpi radialis brevis, which lies more lateral.

Fig. xii, 4.

The *extensor retinaculum ligament* is represented by an oblique band, about 1 inch broad, which extends from the lower part of the outer border of the radius to the styloid process of the ulna and the carpal bones below the ulna. The ligament has,

Fig. xii, 1.

FIG. XII.

1. The extensor retinaculum.
2. Synovial sheath for the abductor and extensor pollicis brevis tendons.
3. Sheath for the extensor carpi radialis longus and brevis tendons.
4. Dorsal tubercle.
5. Sheath for extensor pollicis longus tendons.
6. Sheath for extensor digitorum and indicis tendon.
7. Sheath for extensor digiti minimi.
8. Sheath for extensor carpi ulnaris.
9. Radial artery, cutting across the "anatomical snuff-box."
10. Radial artery dipping down between the two heads of the first dorsal interosseous muscle.
11. The method of insertion of an extensor tendon, to the bases of the middle and distal phalanges.
12. Transverse lines corresponding to the levels of the metacarpo-phalangeal and inter-phalangeal joints.

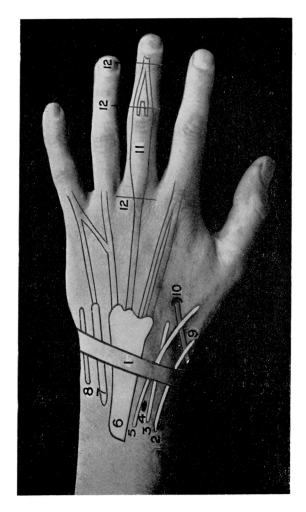

FIG. XII.

To face p. 28.

therefore, a downward and inward direction, and beneath it pass the extensor tendons. These occupy distinct compartments, and possess synovial sheaths as under :

1. One compartment and synovial sheath for the abductor pollicis and extensor pollicis brevis.

Fig. xii, 2.

2. One for the extensor carpi radialis longus and brevis.

Fig. xii, 3.

3. One for the extensor pollicis longus.

Fig. xii, 5.

4. One for the extensor (communis) digitorum and extensor indicis.

Fig. xii, 6.

5. One for the extensor digiti minimi.

Fig. xii, 7.

6. One for the extensor carpi ulnaris.

Fig. xii, 8.

The extent of the synovial sheaths is indicated in the diagram, where the radial artery is also depicted as it crosses the " anatomical snuff-box " towards the base of the first interosseous space, at

Fig. xii, 9, 10.

which level the vessel dips down between the two heads of the first dorsal interosseous muscle to complete the deep palmar arch.

The bony prominence on the medial aspect of the dorsum of the lower end of the ulna alters with pronation and supination of the forearm. In pronation this prominence is formed by the head of the ulna, while in supination the prominence is formed by the styloid process of the ulna

VESSELS, ETC., OF THE UPPER LIMB

The _axillary artery_ extends from the outer border of the first rib to the lower margin of the teres major muscle. When the arm is held out at right angles to the long axis of the body, and the palmar surface of the hand turned upwards, the artery corresponds in direction to a line drawn from the middle of the clavicle to the junction of the anterior and middle thirds of the outer axillary wall at the outlet of that space. At its termination the artery and the accompanying nerves— the neuro-vascular bundle —form a projection which lies behind that due to the coracobrachialis and biceps (short head) muscles. The artery is divided into three parts by the pectoralis minor muscle, which muscle can be represented by a triangle, the base corresponding to the anterior extremities of the third, fourth and fifth ribs, whilst the apex is situated at the end of the coracoid process.

The *brachial artery*.—The arm and forearm being held **Fig. vi, 4.** in the position already indicated as necessary in order to map out the axillary artery, the brachial artery corresponds to a line drawn from the outer wall of the axillary outlet at the junction of its anterior and middle thirds to the mid-point in front of the bend of the elbow at the level of the head of the radius. At the last point the artery bifurcates into radial and ulnar arteries.

The *radial artery* extends from the middle of the bend **Fig. vi, 5.** of the elbow at the level of the head of the radius to the radial side of the tendon of the flexor carpi radialis muscle just above the base of the thumb. The artery then crosses the "anatomical snuff-box" towards the base of the first interosseous space.

The *ulnar artery* in the lower two-thirds of its course **Fig. vi, 6.** accompanies and lies to the lateral side of the ulnar nerve. The upper third of its course is represented by a line which passes obliquely upwards and outwards to the middle of the bend of the elbow at the level of the head of the radius.

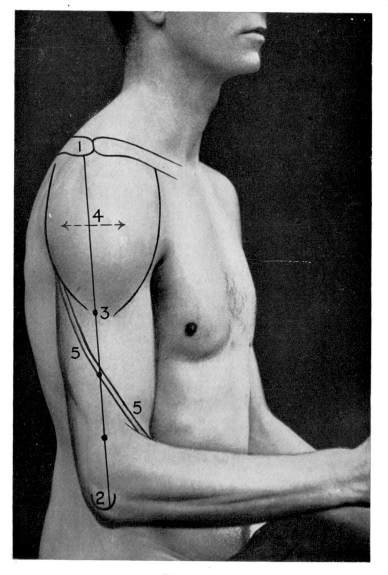

FIG. XIII.

1. The acromion.
2. The lateral epicondyle of the humerus. (Between these two points the length of the humerus may be measured.)
3. The insertion of the deltoid muscle.
4. The mid-point of the deltoid, corresponding to the position of the circumflex nerve and circumflex arteries.
5. 5. The radial nerve.

To face p. 31.

The *superficial palmar arch* is formed by the anastomosis
Fig. x, 8. of the superficial division of the ulnar artery
with the superficial palmar branch, or some
other branch, of the radial artery. The convexity of the
arch looks towards the fingers, and lies on a level with the
lower border of the outstretched thumb. Occasionally
the arch extends lower down, reaching as far as the upper
of the two transverse creases on the palmar aspect of the
hand.

The *deep palmar arch*, formed by the anastomosis of the
Fig. x, 10. radial artery with the deep branch of the ulnar,
lies about one finger's breadth proximal to the
level of the superficial palmar arch.

The *digital branches* of the superficial palmar arch pass
Fig. x, 9. downwards in the intervals between the metacarpal bones to within ½ inch of the digital
clefts, where the vessels bifurcate to run along the
adjacent sides of the fingers.

The digital nerves bifurcate proximally to the deep
transverse metacarpal ligament, whereas the arteries
divide distally.

The *circumflex nerve and the posterior circumflex artery*
Fig. xiii, 4. pass backwards through the quadrilateral
space (teres minor and subscapularis above,
teres major below, long head of triceps medially, and
humerus laterally), and curl round the surgical neck of the
humerus, towards the outer and anterior aspect of the
shoulder region. The artery anastomoses with the anterior
circumflex artery, and the level of the arterial circle so
formed, and of the *circumflex nerve*, may be represented
by a line drawn at right angles to the shaft of the humerus
from a point just above the centre of the deltoid muscle.

The *musculo-cutaneous nerve* usually pierces the inner

aspect of the coracobrachialis muscle about 1 to 2 inches below the coracoid process. It then runs downwards and outwards, deep to the biceps muscle, towards the outer bicipital sulcus, at which level it becomes cutaneous. The course of the nerve in the arm can, therefore, be roughly indicated by a line from the coracoid process above to the outer bicipital sulcus below.

The *radial nerve*, accompanied by the anterior branch of the profunda brachii artery, pierces the lateral intermuscular septum of the arm, from behind forwards, at the junction of the upper and middle thirds of a line drawn from the insertion of the deltoid muscle to the lateral epicondyle of the humerus. Below this point the nerve passes downwards and inwards to the outer bicipital sulcus, where it gives origin to its posterior interosseous branch. Above the point at which the nerve pierces the lateral intermuscular septum, its course may be represented by a curved line drawn upwards and inwards to the junction of the upper arm with the posterior fold of the axilla.

Fig. xiii, 5.

From the outer bicipital sulcus, the *radial nerve* is continued down the forearm, accompanying, and lying to the outer side of, the radial artery in its middle third. At the junction of the middle and lower thirds of the forearm, the nerve turns round the outer border of the radius under cover of the brachioradialis tendon, to be distributed to the back of the wrist and hand.

Fig. vi, 2.

The *posterior interosseous* nerve is given off from the radial in the outer bicipital sulcus, and curls round the neck of the radius in the substance of the supinator muscle, emerging from the posterior border of that muscle 2 inches below the head of the radius. It then passes down the posterior aspect of the forearm, lying about midway between the inner and outer borders, and terminating in a gangliform enlargement at the posterior aspect of the wrist.

The *median nerve in the arm.*—This nerve accompanies the brachial artery, and therefore presents a similar surface marking. It is necessary, however, to bear in mind that the nerve crosses the artery superficially from above downwards and from without inwards.

Fig. vi, 7.

The *median nerve* in the forearm passes downwards from the inner bicipital sulcus to the front of the wrist, there lying to the medial side of the flexor carpi radialis and under cover of the palmaris longus tendon. The nerve then passes under the flexor retinaculum to the palm.

Fig. vi, 7.

The *ulnar nerve* in the upper third of the arm lies along the inner side of the brachial artery. It then leaves that vessel, and, accompanied by the ulnar collateral artery, passes downwards and backwards to reach the hollow between the medial epicondyle and the olecranon process.

Fig. vi, 8.

The *ulnar nerve* in the forearm corresponds in direction to a line drawn from the medial epicondyle of the humerus to the medial side of the pisiform bone. In front of the wrist the nerve lies to the medial side of the tendon of the flexor carpi ulnaris muscle, and subsequently passes superficial to the flexor retinaculum, protected by the volar carpal ligament, to its palmar distribution.

Fig. vi, 8.

The *palmar fascia* is triangular in shape, the apex attached to the flexor retinaculum between the thenar and hypothenar eminences, whilst the base corresponds to the proximal ends of the four fingers.

The Creases of the Palm and Fingers.

The proximal transverse crease on the palmar aspect of the hand lies just below the normal limit of the superficial palmar arch, but at the level of the lower limit of the main flexor synovial sheath. The distal crease crosses the necks of the metacarpal bones, and corresponds to the praximal limit of the distal flexor synovial sheaths.

The metacarpo-phalangeal joints lie about half-way between the distal crease of the palm and the proximal crease of the fingers. The middle and distal creases on the palmar aspect of the fingers correspond fairly accurately to the respective interphalangeal joints. The " knuckles " are formed by the *heads* of metacarpal bones.

CHAPTER III

THE THORAX

THE majority of the thoracic viscera are depicted on the surface in relation to the costal cartilages, ribs and intercostal spaces, and it is therefore necessary to lay stress on certain important points :

1. That the twelve ribs are divided into two groups : (a) *True* ribs, seven in number, articulating by means of their costal cartilages with the sterno-xiphoid bone ; (b) *False* ribs, five in number, all falling short of the middle line, the upper three attached to the costal cartilage of the rib above, the lower two *not* articulating with the transverse process of the corresponding vertebral, and the anterior extremities *not* attached to the costal cartilage of the rib above. These last two ribs are therefore known as " floating ribs."

2. That the 1st rib lies mainly under cover of the clavicle, but that its costal cartilage can generally be palpated with ease as it lies below the sternal end of the clavicle.

3. That the 1st interspace which can be felt to the outer side of the sternum *is* the 1st interspace. This axiom may appear at first sight to be quite unnecessary, but it is in reality not uncommon for students to regard the first space which can be felt as the second interspace.

35

4. That the 2nd costal cartilage articulates in front at
Fig. xvii. the sternal angle (of Louis) with the adjoining parts of the manubrium and body of
the sternum.

5. That the 7th costal cartilage articulates with the
Fig. xvii. adjoining parts of the body and xiphoid process.

6. That the anterior extremity of the 9th costal cartilage
Fig. xviii. corresponds almost exactly to the point where
the linea semilunaris cuts the costal arch.

7. That the 12th rib is liable to great variation in size, frequently being so insignificant that it cannot be felt at all. It is, therefore, often advisable to count from above in fixing any particular rib.

8. That the intercostal spaces, in consequence of the downward and forward obliquity of the ribs, are wider in front than behind.

The female *mamma*, when well developed, extends upwards to the 2nd rib, inwards to the outer border of the sternum, downwards to the 6th or 7th rib, and outwards to the mid-axillary line. The true glandular substance is, however, less regular in disposition, roughly resembling in shape the " ace of clubs," the stem—" axillary prolongation "—being directed upwards and outwards along the anterior fold of the axilla.

The *nipple* usually corresponds to the 4th interspace. It is variable in position, and not infrequently overlies the 4th rib. In the female the nipple lies just below, and external to, the apex or central point of the breast.

Fig. xiv. The *heart* lies opposite the middle four
thoracic vertebræ and the projection of its anterior surface upon the front of the chest wall may be indicated in the following manner.

Take the following four points :

1. The lower border of the 2nd left costal cartilage about 1 inch from the left border of the sternum.

2. The upper border of the 3rd right costal cartilage $\frac{1}{4}$ to $\frac{1}{2}$ inch from the right border of the sternum.

3. The lower border of the 6th right costal cartilage $\frac{3}{4}$ inch from the right border of the sternum.

4. The 5th left interspace $1\frac{1}{2}$ inches below and just medial to a line drawn vertically downwards from the nipple. If any abnormality exists with regard to the position of the nipple, this last point may be fixed with greater accuracy by taking a point in the 5th left interspace in the mid-clavicular line.

The apex beat—the point of maximum impulse of the left ventricle against the chest wall—lies in the **Fig. xiv, 8.** 5th left interspace $1\frac{1}{2}$ inches below and $\frac{1}{2}$ inch medial to the nipple, or $3\frac{1}{2}$ inches from the middle line. The position of the apex beat, therefore, does not exactly represent the outermost limit of the left ventricle. The above four points should now be joined in the following manner :

Points 1 and 2 by a straight line.

Points 2 and 3 by a curved line, the heart reaching the greatest distance from the middle line, $1\frac{1}{2}$ inches, in the 4th interspace.

Points 3 and 4 by a line presenting a slight downward convexity, and cutting across the middle line in close relation to the xiphisternal junction.

Points 1 and 4 by a line presenting a fairly well-marked convexity to the left. In the illustration this line is drawn rather too straight.

A line joining Points 1 and 3 divides this cardiac area **Fig. xiv, 5.** into two parts, which roughly correspond to the *auricular* area above and to the right, and

the *ventricular* area below and to the left. This ventricular
area is occupied mainly by the right ventricle,
whilst a narrow strip along the left border
represents that part of the left ventricle which
comes to the surface.

Fig. xiv, 6.

Fig. xiv, 7.

The four points given above for marking out the projection of the heart on the anterior thoracic wall may be
simplified by taking and joining the following four points :

1. The upper border of the 3rd right chondro-sternal
joint.

2. The lower border of the 2nd left chondro-sternal
joint.

3. The lower border of the 6th right chondro-sternal
joint.

4. The position of the apex beat.

By uniting these four points, the heart is mapped out
for most practical purposes, with sufficient accuracy.

THE VALVES OF THE HEART.

1. The *pulmonary* valve is situated at the highest level,
and lies opposite the upper border of the 3rd
left costal cartilage, close to its junction with
the sternum.

Fig. xiv, 9.

2. The *aortic* valve lies just below and medial to the
pulmonary valve at the lower border of the
3rd left costal cartilage at its junction with
the sternum.

Fig. xiv, 11.

3. The *mitral* or left auriculo-ventricular valve is situated behind the left half of the sternum at the
level of the 4th chondro-sternal joint.

Fig. xiv, 12.

4. The *tricuspid* or right auriculo-ventricular valve lies
very obliquely behind the sternum at the level
of the 4th interspace and the anterior extrem-

Fig. xiv, 13.

FIG. XIV.

N.B.—In this and in other figures in which the costal cartilages are depicted the numbered references do *not* refer to the corresponding cartilages. These are numbered for general convenience only.

1–4. The four points of the heart.
5. The auricular area.
6. The ventricular area.
7. The left ventricle.
8. The apex beat.
9. The pulmonary valve.
10. The pulmonary artery.
11. The aortic valve.
12. The mitral valve.
13. The tricuspid valve.
14. The ascending aorta.
15. The aortic arch.
16. The innominate artery.
17. The right and left common carotid arteries.
18. The right and left subclavian arteries.
19. The right and left subclavian veins.
20. The right and left internal jugular veins.
21. The right and left innominate veins.
22. The superior vena cava.
23. The inferior vena cava.
24. The abdominal aorta.
25. The cœliac artery.
26. The superior mesenteric artery.
27. The renal arteries.
28. The inferior mesenteric artery.
29. The common iliac arteries.
30. The internal iliac arteries.
31. The external iliac arteries.
32. The kidney.
33. The ureters
34. The ovary.

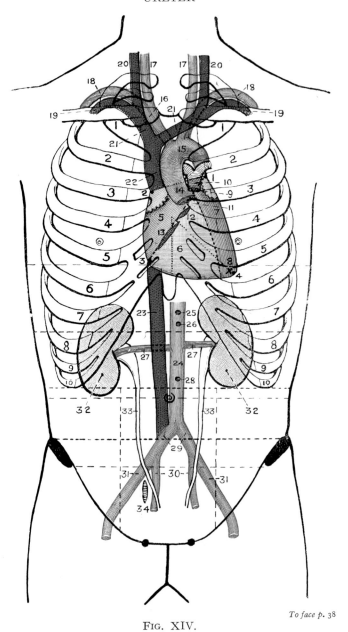

FIG. XIV.

To face p. 38

ities of the 5th costal cartilages, extending downwards and to the right almost as far as the 6th chondro-sternal joint.

The Aorta and other Vessels, etc.

The *ascending aorta*, 2 to 2½ inches long, arises behind
Fig. xiv, 14. the left border of the sternum at the level of the 3rd costal cartilage, and passes upwards and to the right towards the right border of the sternum at the level of the 2nd costal cartilage.

The *aortic arch* is directed backwards and to the left,
Fig. xiv, 15. the upper limit lying about 1 inch below the suprasternal notch, or half-way between that notch and the angle of Louis (junction of manubrium and body of sternum). The arch becomes the descending aorta at the left side of the lower part of the body of the 4th thoracic vertebra.

The *descending thoracic aorta*, 7 to 8 inches long, passes onwards through the posterior mediastinum, and pierces the diaphragm at the level of the 12th dorsal vertebra. The site of diaphragmatic perforation is represented on the surface by a point situated just to the left of the middle line, two fingers' breadth above the transpyloric plane.*

The *innominate artery*, 1½ to 2 inches long, arises from
Fig. xiv, 16. the aortic arch in the middle line 1 inch below the suprasternal notch, and passes upwards and to the right, to the right sternoclavicular joint, at which level it bifurcates into its two terminal branches.

The *left common carotid* (thoracic course) arises from the aortic arch on a posterior plane to, and slightly to the
Fig. xiv, 17. left of, the trunk of the innominate artery, and passes upwards, and to the left, to the left sternoclavicular joint.

* Any " planes " mentioned in this chapter will be explained in the chapter on the abdomen.

4

The *left subclavian artery* (thoracic course) arises from
Fig. xiv, 18. the aortic arch on a posterior plane to, and slightly to the left of, the thoracic part of the left common carotid artery, and passes almost vertically upwards behind the left border of the sternum to the left sternoclavicular joint.

The *superior mediastinum* is bounded above by the plane
Fig. xvii. of the thoracic inlet and below by a plane which passes backwards from the sternal angle in front to the lower border of the 4th thoracic vertebra (Louis's plane).

The *pulmonary artery* arises opposite the upper border
Fig. xiv, 10. of the 3rd left costal cartilage at its junction with the sternum, and passes backwards and slightly upwards to its bifurcation, which takes place opposite the 2nd left costal cartilage.

The *internal mammary artery* arises from the first part
Fig. xx, 8. of the cervical course of the subclavian artery, and passes almost vertically downwards behind the corresponding sternoclavicular joint. In its further thoracic course, the artery lies $\frac{1}{2}$ inch lateral to the outer border of the sternum, bifurcating opposite the
Fig. xx, 9. 10. 6th costal cartilage or the 6th interspace into the *musculophrenic* and *superior epigastric* arteries. The former vessel curves outwards, following the line of the costal arch, whilst the latter passes onwards to enter the sheath of the rectus abdominis muscle.

The *left innominate vein*, 3 inches long, is formed opposite the left sternoclavicular joint, and passes to the right, slightly overlapping the upper part of the aortic
Fig. xiv, 21. arch, and occupying the greater part of the space between the summit of the arch below and the suprasternal notch above.

The *right innominate vein* is formed at the right sternoclavicular joint, and passes obliquely downwards and inwards to meet the corresponding
vein of the opposite side at the lower border of the 1st
right costal cartilage close to its junction with the sternum.

Fig. xiv,
21.

The *superior vena cava*, formed by the junction of the
above two veins, is directed almost vertically
downwards from the lower border of the 1st
right costal cartilage close to its junction with the
sternum, to open into the right auricle of the heart at the
level of the upper border of the 3rd right chondro-sternal
junction.

Fig. xiv,
22.

The *inferior vena cava* enters upon its short intra-
thoracic course, by passing through the
venacaval or quadrate tendinous opening of
the diaphragm at the level of the 8th thoracic vertebra,
opening into the right auricle of the heart opposite the
5th right interspace and the adjoining part of the sternum.

Fig. xiv,
23.

The *vena azygos* drains the whole thoracic wall, except
the first space on the right side and the upper three
spaces on the left. It opens into the superior vena cava
at the level of the lower part of the 2nd right interspace,
curling round the root of the right lung in order to reach
its destination.

The main *aortic intercostal* vessels occupy the costal
groove of a rib as they pass round the chest wall, lying
between the corresponding vein above, and the nerve
below.

The Pleura and Lungs.

1. The *pleural sacs*.—When the shoulders are depressed
the two clavicles lie practically at right angles
to the long axis of the body, and in this

Fig. xv, 5.
Fig. xvi, 4.

position the apices of the pleural sacs extend into the supraclavicular region, lying about $1\frac{1}{2}$ inches above the clavicle under cover of the clavicular head of the sterno-mastoid muscle.

The anterior margin of each sac sweeps downwards and inwards behind the corresponding sternoclavicular joint, the two sacs converging towards the sternal angle (junction of manubrium and body of sternum), at which level they meet one another just to the left of the middle line. They then pass vertically downwards parallel to one another as far as the level of the 4th chondro-sternal junction.

The right sac passes onwards in the same straight line to the 6th or 7th chondro-sternal joint, and then sweeps round the anterior, lateral, and posterior aspects of the chest wall, cutting across—

(1) The upper part of the 8th costal cartilage in the lateral vertical line ;

(2) The 10th rib in the mid-axillary line ;

(3) The 11th rib in the line of the inferior angle of the scapula ;

(4) The 12th rib at the outer border of the sacro-spinalis muscle.

The obliquity of the 12th rib causes the pleura to fall below the level of the inner half of the rib, the pleura in this last part of its course being directed inwards towards the spine of the 12th dorsal vertebra.

The *left pleura*, from the level of the 4th left chondro-sternal joint, sweeps obliquely outwards and downwards behind the costal cartilages of the 5th, 6th and 7th ribs to the 8th costal cartilage in the lateral vertical plane. Beyond this point the left pleura follows the same general direction as the right sac, descending, however, to a slightly lower level.

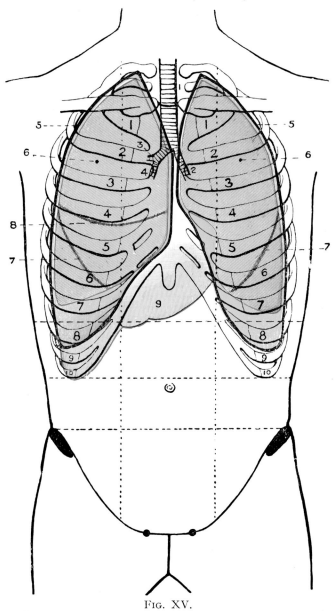

FIG. XV.

1. The trachea.
2. The left bronchus.
3. The eparterial bronchus.
4. The hyparterial bronchus.
5. The pleuræ.
6. The lungs.

7, 7. The main obliquefis-
    sure of the lungs.
8. The small transverse fis-
    sure of the right lung.
9. The liver.
10. Area of superficial cardiac
    dullness.

To face p. 42.

The lowest limit reached by the two pleural sacs is situated in the mid-axillary line, the sacs there cutting across the 10th rib about 2 inches above the costal margin, which is in this situation usually represented by the tip of the 11th rib.

Difficulty is sometimes experienced in endeavouring to verify the position of the 12th thoracic spine, and in such cases the pleural reflection behind the mid-axillary region may be represented by a line which passes almost transversely backwards towards the middle line of the back from the 10th rib in the mid-axillary line.

The two sacs are for the most part separated from one
Fig. xvi, 4. another by the width of the vertebral bodies—about 1½ inches. In the lower part of the posterior mediastinum, however, the right sac approaches the middle line.

2. The *lungs* may be mapped out in part by lines similar to those given for the pleural sacs. The apex of
Fig. xv, 6. the upper lobe of each lung extends into the
Fig. xvi, 5. supraclavicular region, and the anterior margins converge towards the sternal angle, cutting obliquely across the corresponding sternoclavicular joint.

The two anterior borders do not, however, meet at the sternal angle, for the right lung on reaching the middle line passes vertically downwards as far as the level of the 6th or 7th chondro-sternal joint, whilst the left lung runs down behind the left border of the sternum to the junction of the 4th costal cartilage with the sternum. The *right lung*, from the level of the 6th or 7th chondro-sternal joint, sweeps outwards, cutting across—

(1) The 6th costal cartilage in the lateral vertical line ;
(2) The 8th rib in the mid-axillary line ;
(3) The 10th rib in the line of the inferior angle of the

scapula, and finally passing inwards towards the 10th thoracic spine.

The *left lung*, from the outer border of the sternum at the level of the 4th chondro-sternal joint, passes outwards for a short distance along the lower border of the 4th costal cartilage, and then turns downwards and inwards in a curved direction to the 6th costal cartilage in the lateral vertical plane. The lung then sweeps round the chest wall, following a course similar to that already indicated as pursued by the right lung, the left lung lying, however, at a slightly lower level.

Stress should, perhaps, be laid on the fact that, as the lower border of each lung sweeps round the antero-lateral, lateral, and posterior aspects of the chest wall, from the 6th costal cartilage in front to the 10th thoracic spine behind, the course pursued is practically transverse to the long axis of the body.

It will be convenient to put here in a tabulated manner the *comparative lower levels of the right pleura and lung*. Starting in each case at the 6th right chondro-sternal joint, the pleura and lung may be represented by lines which traverse the chest wall, cutting across the—

		Pleura.		Lung.
(1) Lateral vertical plane	.	8th costal cartilage	.	6th costal cartilage
(2) Mid-axillary line	. .	10th rib	.	8th rib
(3) Scapular line	. . .	11th rib	.	10th rib
(4) and sweeping inwards towards the	. . .	12th spine	.	10th spine.

The numbers to be remembered are, therefore, 6, 8, 10, 11, and 12 for the *pleura*, and 6, 6, 8, 10, 10 for the *lung*.

On the left side, the levels are similar with two main exceptions—(*a*) the lung and pleura sweep outwards so as to leave a part of the heart uncovered (see " *superficial*

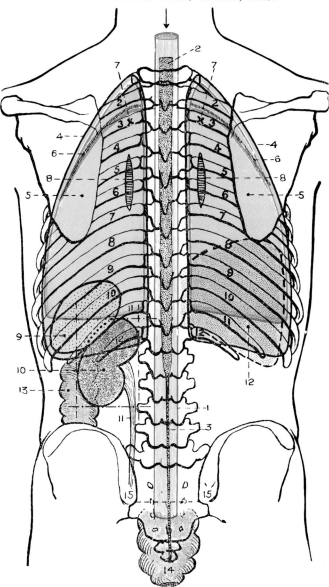

Fig. XVI.

1, 1. The spinal dural sheath.
2. The spinal cord.
3. The filum terminale.
4, 4. The pleuræ.
5, 5. The lungs.
6, 6. The main oblique fissures of the lungs.
7, 7. The apex of the lower lobe of the lungs.
8, 8. The roots of the lungs.

9. The spleen.
10. The left kidney in Morris's parallelogram.*
11. The ureter.
12. The liver.
13. The descending colon.
14. The rectum.
15. The posterior superior iliac spine.

* The transverse processes of the first and second lumbar vertebræ should be drawn in such a manner as to come into contact with the inner border of the kidney.

To face p. 44.

cardiac dullness "), (*b*) both lung and pleura descend to a slightly lower level.

The Lower Limit of the Lung, the Pleura, and the Liver in the Right Mid-axillary Line.

(1) The lung corresponds to the   *8th rib*.
(2)   ,, pleura   ,,   ,,   *10th rib*.
(3)   ,, liver   ,,   ,,   *costal margin*, or even
                                        lower.

The fissures of the lungs.—The main fissure of each lung
Fig. xv, 7.   is indicated by a curved line which starts
Fig. xvi, 6. behind at the level of the *2nd thoracic spine*,
the apex of the main lower lobe of each lung, therefore, being situated immediately below and lateral to this thoracic spine. When the arms fall naturally to the side of the body, the line representing the main fissure cuts across the infraspinous surface of the scapula, and crossing then the 5th rib in the mid-axillary line, terminates in front at the inferior border of the lung at the level of the *6th costochondral joint*. When the arms are extended above the head, the inferior angle of the scapula slides upwards and outwards on the chest wall. In this position the main fissure is represented by a line from the *2nd thoracic spine* which passes downwards and outwards to the inferior angle of the scapula, and then forwards to the termination of the fissure at the inferior border of the lung.

The smaller or transverse fissure of the right lung separates off from the main fissure in the mid-axillary line,
Fig. xv, 8.   and passes almost transversely forwards along
            the lower border of the *4th rib and costal cartilage* to the anterior border of the lung. It is thus manifest that the anterior aspect of the chest, above the level of the *6th costal cartilage*, corresponds to the upper

two lobes of the right lung and to the upper lobe of the left lung, whilst the posterior aspect of the chest below the level of the 2nd thoracic spine corresponds to the right and left main lower lobes.

The *apices of the upper and lower lobes.*—It will be here in place to again lay stress on the fact that the *apex of the upper main lobe* lies about 1 inch above the clavicle in the supraclavicular fossa, under cover of the clavicular head of a well-developed sternomastoid muscle, and that the apex of the lower lobe lies immediately below and lateral to the spine of the 2nd thoracic vertebra.

Fig. xv.
Fig. xvi, 7.

The *roots of the lungs* lie opposite the spines of the 4th, 5th and 6th thoracic vertebræ, and the bodies of the 5th, 6th and 7th. They may be so represented, lying also midway between the middle line of the back and the vertebral border of the scapula, the arms hanging loosely from the shoulders.

Fig. xvi,
8.

The *areas of deep and superficial cardiac dullness.*—

1. The area of *deep cardiac dullness*, quadrate in form, corresponds to the complete area already mapped out as representing the projection of the heart on to the anterior aspect of the chest wall.

Fig. xiv,
1-4.

2. The area of *superficial cardiac dullness*, more or less triangular in shape, corresponds to that part of the heart which is not covered by the thin anterior margin of the lung. This area can, with sufficient accuracy, be defined as a triangular space, the left border being formed by a line from the 4th left chondro-sternal joint to the apex beat of the heart in the 5th left interspace, the right border by a line which passes downwards along the middle of the sternum from the level of the anterior extremities of the 4th to 7th costal cartilages,

Fig. xv,
10.

and the base by a line which passes laterally from the level of the 7th costal cartilage to the position of the apex beat.

A reference to Figs. xiv and xv will make it evident that *paracentesis of the pericardium* can be performed, without injury to pleura or lung, in the 5th left intercostal space. The internal mammary artery runs vertically downwards about ½ inch from the outer border of the sternum, and the needle should, therefore, be inserted through the 5th intercostal space about 1 inch from the outer border of the sternum.

The *trachea and bronchi.*—The trachea, 4½ inches long, Fig. xv, 1. commences immediately below the cricoid cartilage, on a level with the 6th cervical vertebra, and passing downwards through the superior mediastinum, *bifurcates opposite the level of the lower part of the body of the 4th thoracic vertebra* (Louis's plane).

The two bronchi diverge, the left being the longer Fig. xv, 2, and the narrower. The tendency of foreign 3, 4. bodies to pass more frequently into the right bronchus is explained by the fact that the septum between the two bronchi is placed to the left of the middle line of the trachea. The right bronchus, previous to the giving-off of the eparterial bronchus, is less obliquely inclined than the left bronchus, though subsequently it follows much the same course.

The greater obliquity of the left bronchus accounts also for the fact that the left pulmonary artery tends to lie at the higher level, whilst the right pulmonary artery lies below the level of the corresponding bronchus.

The *œsophagus*, 9 inches long, also commences at the Fig. xix, level of the cricoid cartilage, and passing 1, 1. downwards through the superior and posterior mediastina, pierces the diaphragm at the level of the

10th thoracic vertebra, entering the stomach at the level of the 11th thoracic vertebra.

The entrance of the œsophagus into the stomach may be indicated by taking a point on the 7th left costal cartilage ½ inch away from the left side of the xiphisternal joint.

The *thoracic duct*, 15 to 18 inches long, commences at the cisterna chyli, a spindle-shaped sac which lies **Fig. xx, 5.** opposite the bodies of the 1st and 2nd lumbar vertebræ, and between the thoracic aorta on the left and the lumbar azygos on the right. It may be represented on the surface by an oval enlargement placed just to the right of the middle line, occupying the upper two-thirds of the space between the transpyloric (1st lumbar) and subcostal (3rd lumbar) planes.

The efferent duct pierces the diaphragm through the **Fig. xx, 6.** aortic orific opposite the 12th thoracic vertebra, and passes almost vertically upwards through the posterior mediastinum, just to the right of the middle line, as far as the lower part of the 4th thoracic vertebra (Louis's plane). The duct now crosses behind the œsophagus to the left of the middle line, and then again passes vertically upwards through the superior mediastinum and into the neck as far as the level of the transverse process of the 7th cervical vertebra. Finally the duct curls outwards and downwards to open into the **Fig. xx, 7.** angle between the internal jugular and subclavian veins of the left side. The duct drains the whole of the lymphatic area of the body, except the right side of the head and neck, the right arm, the right side of the thorax and the convexity of the liver, the lymphatics from these regions draining into a smaller duct which opens into the angle between the right internal jugular and subclavian veins.

CHAPTER IV

THE ABDOMEN

THE anterior aspect of the trunk (*i.e.* thorax and abdomen)
is divisible into right and left halves by a
median vertical plane from the middle point at
the suprasternal notch above to the pubic symphysis
below. Each half is again divided by a *lateral vertical
plane* which is drawn parallel to the median
plane, half-way between that plane and the
anterior superior iliac spine. Prolonged downwards, this
lateral plane crosses the inguinal (Poupart's) ligament
rather nearer to the medial than to the lateral end.
Prolonged upwards, it crosses the clavicle about midway
between the median point at the suprasternal notch and
the acromioclavicular joint.

That part of the lateral vertical plane which traverses
the mammary region is sometimes called the "mammary
plane," that part which crosses the clavicle the "clavicular
plane," and the downward prolongation which cuts across
the inguinal ligament the "Poupart plane."

The clavicular, mammary, and Poupart planes are,
however, continuous, and they together form the *lateral
vertical plane*, which is chosen in preference to the mid-
Poupart plane of many anatomists, since it is measured
from the median plane to a fixed bony point. Two
vertical planes only will be consequently retained in
the subdivision of the anterior aspect of the trunk—the
median and lateral vertical planes.

Fig. xvii, 3, 3.

Fig. xvii, 4, 4.

49

The median plane can be bisected by a horizontal plane which is on the same level as the body of the first lumbar vertebra.　This plane so constantly cuts across the pyloric end of the stomach that it is called the *transpyloric plane*

Fig. xvii.

(of Addison), and it will be found that not only does this plane lie half-way between the suprasternal notch and the pubic symphysis, but that it also lies midway between the umbilicus and the xiphisternal joint.　It is, therefore, not necessary to expose the whole of the anterior aspect of the trunk in order to verify the position of the transpyloric plane—a plane of the greatest value in defining the position of several abdominal viscera.

The point at which the *median vertical* and *transpyloric*

Fig. xvii, 1.

planes intersect has been suitably called the " central point," and the point of intersection of the *lateral vertical* and *transpyloric planes* may be

Fig. xvii, 2.

tentatively called the " lateral central " or " paracentral " point.　This latter point usually corresponds to the anterior extremity of the ninth costal cartilage.

The distance between the " central point " and the top of the pubic symphysis is bisected by a horizontal plane

Fig. xvii.

which passes through the tubercles of the iliac crests, the *transtubercular plane*, a plane corresponding to the level of the body of the fifth lumbar vertebra.　It has also been suggested that the distance between the " central point " and the suprasternal notch should likewise be bisected by a plane—the *thoracic plane* —which crosses the body of the sternum at the level of some part of the anterior extremities of the fourth costal

Fig. xvii.

cartilages.　This plane is, however, of little value, and is merely mentioned as completing

Level of hard palate = 1st cervical.
Level of free margin of upper teeth = 2nd cervical.
Level of hyoid bone = 2nd to 3rd cervical.
Level of upper part of thyroid cartilage = 4th cervical.
Level of cricoid cartilage = 6th cervical.

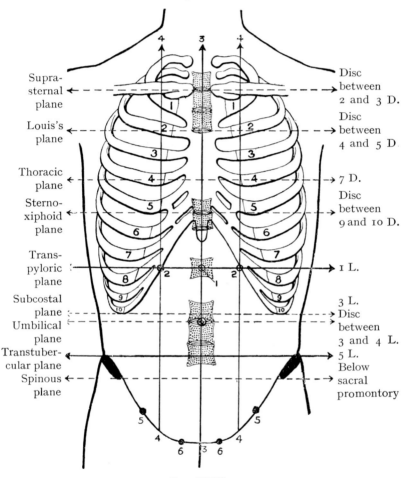

Supra-sternal plane ← − − − − − − − − − − → Disc between 2 and 3 D.

Louis's plane ← − − − − − − − − − − → Disc between 4 and 5 D.

Thoracic plane ← − − − − − − − − − − → 7 D.

Sterno-xiphoid plane ← − − − − − − − − − → Disc between 9 and 10 D.

Trans-pyloric plane ← − − − − − − − − − − → 1 L.

Subcostal plane ← − − − − − − − − − → 3 L.
Umbilical plane ← − − − − − − − − − → Disc between 3 and 4 L.
Transtuber-cular plane ← − − − − − − − − − → 5 L.
Spinous plane ← − − − − − − − − − → Below sacral promontory

FIG. XVII.

1.   The central point.
2, 2. The lateral central or paracentral point.
3, 3. The median vertical plane.
4, 4. The lateral vertical plane.
5, 5. The mid-point of the inguinal ligament.
6, 6. The pubic spines.

To face p. 50.

the symmetrical subdivision of the median vertical plane into four equal parts.

The following planes are, therefore, chosen as the most scientific in the subdivision of the anterior aspect of the trunk :

Two vertical planes—(1) The median ; (2) the lateral.

Three transverse planes—(1) The transtubercular ; (2) the transpyloric ; (3) the thoracic.

Two important points are also named—(1) The central point ; (2) the lateral central point.

The abdominal regions mapped out by the intersection of the transpyloric and transtubercular planes with the lateral vertical planes receive the same nomenclature as in the older methods of regional subdivision of the abdomen. These regions are nine in number :

Fig. xviii. 1. Right hypochondriac. 2. Epigastric. 3. Left hypochondriac. 4. Right lumbar. 5. Umbilical. 6. Left lumbar. 7. Right iliac. 8. Hypogastric. 9. Left iliac.

OTHER TRANSVERSE PLANES, WITH THEIR CORRESPONDING VERTEBRAL LEVELS.

Fig. xvii. (a) The *suprasternal plane*, on a level with the disc between the 2nd and 3rd thoracic vertebræ.

(b) *Louis's plane* (junction of manubrium and body of the sternum), on a level with the disc between the 4th and 5th thoracic vertebræ.*

(c) The *sterno-xiphoid plane* (junction of sternum and xiphoid process), on a level with the disc between the 9th and 10th thoracic vertebræ.

* The manubrium and body of the sternum unite at an angle, known as the sternal angle (Louis).

(*d*) The *subcostal plane*, on a level with the lower part of the 3rd lumbar vertebra.

(*e*) The *umbilical plane*, on a level with the disc between the 3rd and 4th lumbar vertebræ.

(*f*) The *spinous plane*, drawn between the two anterior superior iliac spines, and usually falling below the level of the sacral promontory.

The *lineæ semilunares* corresponds to the lateral border
Fig. xviii, of the rectus abdominis muscle, and extends,
7. with a slight outward convexity, from the pubic tubercle below to the tip of the 9th costal cartilage above (the lateral central point).

The *lineæ transversæ* result from the tendinous inter-
Fig. xviii, sections in the rectus abdominis muscle. They
8. are three in number, and are situated—(1) at the level of the umbilicus; (2) midway between the umbilicus and the xiphoid cartilage; (3) immediately below the xiphoid cartilage.

The *arcuate line* (semilunar fold of Douglas), represent-
Fig. xviii, ing the lower limit of the posterior lamella of
9. the rectus sheath, lies about half-way between the umbilicus and the upper border of the pubic symphysis.

The *umbilicus* usually lies 1 to 1½ inches above the
Fig. xviii, transtubercular plane, and corresponds to the
4. level of the disc between the 3rd and 4th lumbar vertebræ. The umbilicus is, however, so inconstant in position that the umbilical plane is rejected as often as possible in favour of a more definite and scientific plane.

The *iliac spines and crest.*—When the body is in the dorsal recumbent position, the anterior superior iliac spine is usually visible to the eye, and no palpation is needful in order to fix its position. In the obese, however, it is

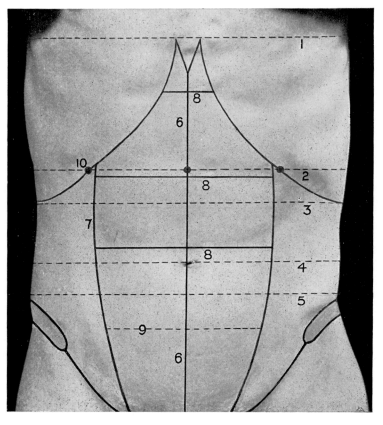

FIG. XVIII.

1. Sterno-xiphoid plane.
2. Transpyloric plane.
3. Subcostal plane.
4. Umbilical plane.
5. Transtubercular plane.
6. Linea alba.

7. Linea semilunaris.
8. Lineæ transversæ.
9. Arcuate line (semilunar fold of Douglas).
10. Anterior renal point.

To face p. 52.

generally necessary to trace forward the iliac crest to its anterior termination. By tracing the iliac crests in a backward direction the " iliac tubercles " will be found, lying about 2 to 2½ inches behind the anterior superior spines, and a line uniting these two tubercles (*the trans-tubercular plane*) corresponds to the level of the 5th lumbar vertebra. Posterior to these tubercles the iliac crests rise to a higher level, so that a line passing round the body at the *highest* level of the crests cuts the middle line of the back at the level of the interspace between the laminæ of the 3rd and 4th lumbar vertebræ (see " *lumbar puncture* " p. 67). Still further backward, the posterior superior iliac spines will be found at the posterior termination of the

Fig. xxi, 1. iliac crest. A line which joins the posterior superior iliac spines cuts across the spine of the 2nd sacral vertebra.

The *pubic tubercle* lies at the lateral extremity of the

Fig. xvii, 6, 6. pubic crest. In the male it is advisable to invaginate the scrotum in order to locate the position of this tubercle ; whilst in the female, owing to the prominence of the mons pubis, it is usually necessary to abduct the thigh, to feel for the rounded tendon of the adductor longus muscle, and to trace this tendon up to its origin from a depression on the pubic bone, which is situated immediately below and internal to the pubic tubercle.

In the erect position of the body the pubic symphysis is nearly horizontal, the inner or pelvic surface looking upwards and only slightly backwards, whilst the external surface faces downwards and a little forwards. The pubic crest is therefore practically directed forwards and the pubic arch backwards. A knife inserted horizontally backwards immediately above the pubic symphysis would pass above the upper limit of the prostate gland and below the promontory of the sacrum ; whilst if directed horizontally backwards below the pubic symphysis, it would pierce the prostate near its centre and pass below the level of the tip of the coccyx.

The *inguinal canal.*—In the adult this canal is about
1½ inches long, and extends from the deep
to the superficial inguinal rings. The *deep
inguinal ring*, a funnel-shaped prolongation of the transversalis fascia, is situated ½ inch above the mid-point of the inguinal ligament. The *superficial inguinal ring*, formed by the splitting of the aponeurosis of the external oblique muscle, is triangular in shape, the base directed downwards and inwards and opening up immediately above the pubic tubercle, whilst the apex is directed upwards and outwards.

Fig. xx, 19,
19.
Fig. xx, 17,
17.

Fig. xx, 18,
18.

The *lumbar triangle* (triangle of Petit).—This triangle is bounded anteriorly by the posterior border of the external oblique, and posteriorly by the anterior border of the latissimus dorsi muscle, whilst the base is formed by part of the iliac crest. The external oblique is inserted into the anterior half of the iliac crest, and the base of the triangle corresponds to 1 to 2 inches of the bone behind the mid-point of the crest. The triangle is subject to great variation in size, the two bounding muscles converging rapidly above to form the apex of the triangle. The floor is formed by the internal oblique muscle.

THE ALIMENTARY CANAL.

The *stomach.*—Capacity about 2 pints. The *cardiac orifice* lies opposite the 11th thoracic vertebra, and is situated about 4 inches away from the surface. It corresponds in position to a point on the 7th costal cartilage ½ inch away from the lateral border of

Fig. xix, 2.

the xiphisternal joint. The seventh costal cartilage is the lowest of the series of cartilages which articulate in front with the central xiphersternal bar, and forms, therefore, the upper lateral boundary of the epigastric triangle. The *pyloric orifice* lies opposite the 1st lumbar vertebra, and corresponds in position to a point in the transpyloric plane just to the right of the middle line.

Fig. xix, 3.

The *lesser curvature* is represented by a curved line, convexity to the left, uniting the above two points. The *greater curvature*, in the moderately distended condition of the stomach, ascends to the lower border of the left 5th costal cartilage and rib, lying immediately above and behind the apex of the heart. Sweeping then downwards the greater curvature usually cuts the left costal margin at some part of the 9th costal cartilage, and finally curves upwards and inwards to the pylorus. The upper limit of the fundus of the stomach corresponds to the level of the left dome of the diaphragm. Thus the stomach may be represented diagrammatically, but owing to the changes in shape which it undergoes during digestion, it is impossible to indicate its appearance and dimensions on the surface with any real accuracy. After barium X-ray, it appears more as a vertical tube, the lower border, before turning up to the pylorus, descending to the level of, or below, the umbilical plane. Perhaps it suffices to indicate the two more or less fixed points, cardiac and pyloric orifices, and to draw a somewhat U-shaped organ between the two.

Fig. xix, 3.

The *duodenum.*—Total length, about 10 inches. Part 1 = 2 inches; part 2 = 3 to 4 inches; part 3 = 4 to 5 inches.

Fig. xix, 4, 4, 4.

The pyloric orifice of the stomach lies opposite the 1st

5

lumbar vertebra, and the first part of the duodenum is directed backwards, with a slight inclination upwards to the right side of the body of the 1st lumbar vertebra.

Part 2 descends, on the right side of the median vertical plane, from the level of the 1st lumbar vertebra (transpyloric plane) to the level of the 3rd lumbar vertebra (subcostal plane). The third part of the duodenum passes almost transversely across the middle line at the level of the subcostal plane, and having reached the left side of the middle line, ascends sharply to the *duo-*
Fig. xix, 5. *denojejunal* flexure, which is placed on a level with the 2nd lumbar vertebra, just below the transpyloric plane, and 1 to 1½ inches to the left of the middle line. The duodenum is subject to great variation in position, and the description given merely represents the average situation of this loop of the small gut. The pyloric orifice of the stomach and the duodenojejunal flexure are both fairly constant in position, and between these two more or less fixed points the gut describes a loop which varies both in shape and in extent.

The *pancreas.*—The head of the pancreas occupies the concavity of the duodenal loop, the body cross-
Fig. xix, 4′. ing the middle line at the level of the 1st and 2nd lumbar vertebræ, and occupying, therefore, the upper two-thirds of the space between the transpyloric (1st lumbar) and subcostal (3rd lumbar) planes. The tail of the pancreas extends to the left as far as the hilum of the spleen.

The *small intestine* is about 23 feet in length, the upper-two-fifths being known as the jejunum, the lower three-fifths as the ileum.

The *mesenteric attachment* of the small gut extends from a point 1 to 1½ inches to the left of the middle
Fig. xix, 6. line, and just below the transpyloric plane

FIG. XIX.

1, 1. The œsophagus.
2. The stomach.
3. The pylorus.
4, 4, 4. The three parts of the duodenum. 4'. The pancreas.
5. The duodenojejunal flexure.
6. The attachment of the mesentery of the small intestine.
7. The ileocolic valve.
8. The cæcum.
9. The vermiform appendix.
10. The ascending colon.
11. The right colic flexure.
12. The left colic flexure.
13. The descending colon.
14. The iliac colon.
15. The ilio-pelvic colon.
16. The lesser omentum (gastro-hepatic).
17. The aditus to the lesser sac (foramen of Winslow).
18. The common bile-duct.

N.B.—The transverse colon has been intentionally omitted.

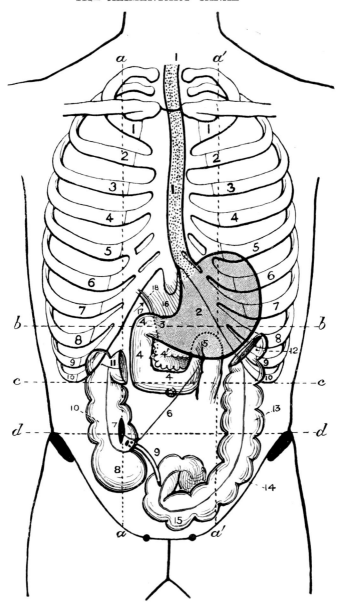

FIG. XIX.

a, a. and *a′, a′* = the lateral vertical planes.
b,·b. The transpyloric plane.
c, c. The subcostal plane.
d, d. The transtubercular plane.

To face p. 56.

(duodenojejunal flexure), to the junction of the right lateral vertical and transtubercular planes. The line drawn between these two points should pass at first obliquely outwards and downwards to the right iliac fossa, curving finally outwards to the region of the ileocolic valve.

The *ileocolic valve* is placed opposite the junction of the right lateral vertical and transtubercular planes.

Fig. xix, 7.

The *cæcum* is about 2½ inches long, and the long axis of the sac is directly downwards, forwards, and inwards. This blind end of the large gut lies below the level of the transtubercular plane, and occupies the right iliac fossa and part of the right half of the hypogastric region.

Fig. xix, 8.

The *vermiform appendix.*—The opening of the appendix into the cæcum is situated just below and medial to the junction of the right lateral vertical and transtubercular planes, at the top right-hand corner of the hypogastric region. The surface marking of the cæcal orifice of the appendix does not coincide with McBurney's point, which is situated at the junction of the outer and middle thirds of a line drawn from the right anterior superior iliac spine to the umbilicus (spino-umbilical line). This point represents the usual seat of maximum pain on palpation in an attack of appendicitis. The appendix is usually 3 to 4 inches long, and is directed downwards and inwards, overhanging the pelvic brim, upwards and inwards towards the spleen, or vertically upwards behind the cæcum. Stress should be laid on the fact that the ileocolic valve and the cæcal orifice of the appendix are both situated on the postero-medial aspect of the cæcum.

Fig. xix, 9.

The *ascending colon* passes upwards from the level of
the transtubercular plane to the upper part of
the 9th right costal cartilage, the gut there
turning on itself to form the *right colic* flexure.   In its
upward course the ascending colon lies almost entirely
to the right of the right lateral vertical plane.

Fig. xix,
10.

The *transverse colon* extends from the *right colic* flexure
on the right to the *left colic* flexure on the left.
The former flexure corresponds to the 9th
costal cartilage, whilst the latter reaches upwards as high
as the 8th.   In between these two points the gut varies
greatly in direction in different subjects.   Most commonly
the gut passes almost transversely from one side to the
other, crossing the middle line at about the level of the 2nd
lumbar vertebra.   It also crosses the second part of the
duodenum, and lies, therefore, usually above
the umbilical plane.   In the diagram the two
flexures are depicted, but the intervening portion of the
gut has been omitted intentionally.

Fig. xix,
11.

Fig. xix,
12.

The *descending colon* passes almost vertically downwards
from the region of the left colic flexure to the
level of the posterior part of the iliac crest,
below which level it becomes known as the *iliac colon*.
The descending colon lies wholly to the left of the left
lateral vertical plane.

Fig. xix,
13.

The operation of lumbar colostomy is now seldom
performed, but it is nevertheless necessary to
indicate the position of the descending colon
on the posterior aspect of the trunk.   It corresponds in
direction to a line drawn vertically upwards to the tip of
the 12th rib, from a point situated $\frac{1}{2}$ inch behind the
mid-point along the iliac crest between the anterior and
posterior superior iliac spines.

Fig. xvi,
13.

The *iliac and pelvic colon.*—Between the termination of the descending colon at the level of the iliac crest, and the beginning of the rectum proper at the level of the third piece of the sacrum, the large gut describes so varied a course that no definite detailed account can be given of its surface marking. It may, however, be briefly described **Fig. xix,** as passing downwards and inwards from the **14.** level of the iliac crest, parallel to the inguinal ligament, as far as the left side of the pelvic brim (the iliac colon). The gut then forms a great loop (the pelvic **Fig. xix,** colon), which sweeps over to the right side of **15.** the pelvic brim, turning on itself to become the rectum at the level of the 3rd sacral vertebra.

The *rectum.*—A line which unites the two posterior superior iliac spines crosses the spinous process of the second sacral vertebra. The rectum begins at the level of the third sacral vertebra, and may be indicated on the surface by drawing in the gut as starting about $\frac{1}{2}$ to $\frac{3}{4}$ inch below the above-mentioned line, and extending downwards, following the curves of the sacrum and coccyx, to the anal orifice, which is placed about 2 inches below the level of the tip of the coccyx.

The dura mater enclosing the spinal cord (see " *spinal* **Fig. xvi.** *cord* ") reaches downwards to the level of the 3rd sacral vertebra. The spinal dura mater, therefore, terminates at the same level as the rectum begins—a point to be borne in mind in those operations carried out in the sacral region for the exposure of a growth involving the gut in the neighbourhood of the junction of the pelvic colon and the rectum.

THE KIDNEY.

(Length, 4½ inches ; breadth, 2½ inches ; thickness, 1½ inches ; weight, 4½ ounces.)

(*a*) *Anterior surface marking.*—The two kidneys are

Fig. xiv, 32. obliquely placed in such a manner that the superior poles lie 1½ to 2 inches, and the inferior poles 2½ to 3 inches, distant from the middle line. The left kidney lies at a slightly higher level than its fellow, and the hilum is placed just below and medial to the junction of the transpyloric and left lateral vertical planes ; in other words, the hilum of the left kidney lies just medial to the anterior extremity of the 9th costal cartilage. The upper pole lies half-way between the sterno-xiphoid and transpyloric planes, whilst the lower pole corresponds to the subcostal plane. The right kidney does not ascend to quite such a high level, and the inferior pole lies opposite the umbilical plane. The hilum of this kidney also lies just below the level of the hilum of the opposite kidney.

(*b*) *Posterior surface marking.*—*Morris's parallelogram.*

Fig. xvi, 10. —Two vertical lines are drawn at a distance of 1 inch and 3½ inches respectively from the middle line of the back, and two horizontal lines are drawn outwards at the level of the spinous processes of the 11th thoracic and 3rd lumbar vertebræ. In the parallelogram so marked out, the kidneys are drawn, care being taken to place the long axis of each kidney in the required oblique direction.

THE URETERS.

(Length, 10 inches.)

(*a*) *Anterior surface marking.*—The ureter passes nearly

Fig. xiv, 33. vertically downwards from the hilum of the kidney (just below and medial to the junction of the transpyloric and lateral vertical planes, *i.e.* from the tip of the 9th costal cartilage), and dips into the true pelvis in close relation to the bifurcation of the common iliac artery. The intrapelvic course of the ureter is unsuited to any surface marking—it passes downwards, and slightly backwards, towards the spine of the ischium, and then forwards to the base of the bladder.

(*b*) *Posterior surface marking.*—The course of the ureter on the posterior aspect of the trunk can be represented by a line drawn vertically upwards from the posterior superior iliac spine to the level of the spinous process of the 2nd lumbar vertebra.

Fig. xvi, 11.

The *ovary* lies in the angle between the internal and external iliac arteries, immediately below the pelvic brim.

Fig. xiv, 34.

The *urachus* is directed upwards from the apex of the bladder, at the upper border of the pubic symphysis, to the umbilicus.

Fig. xx, 15

ABDOMINAL VESSELS.

The *abdominal aorta.*—The thoracic aorta enters the abdominal cavity by passing through the aortic opening of the diaphragm at the level of the 12th thoracic vertebra. The vessel then changes its name, and the abdominal aorta passes vertically downwards as far as the left side of the body of the 4th lumbar vertebra, at which level it bifurcates into the two common iliac arteries. The course of the vessel may be mapped out on the surface by taking a point about two fingers' breadth above the transpyloric plane and slightly to the left of the middle line, and by drawing a line vertically downwards to a second point situated $\frac{1}{2}$ inch below and to the left of the umbilicus.

Fig. xiv, 24.

The first large vessel which arises from the abdominal aorta is the *cœliac artery*. This trunk is given off at the level of the 12th thoracic vertebra, and divides, after a course of about ½ inch, into three main trunks—the hepatic, splenic, and left gastric arteries.

Fig. xiv, 25.

The *superior mesenteric* (level of disc between the 12th dorsal and the 1st lumbar vertebræ) follows next, springing from the anterior aspect of the aorta immediately above the transpyloric plane.

Fig. xiv, 26.

The *renals* (level of the 1st lumbar vertebra) pass outwards from the lateral aspect of the aorta immediately below the level of the transpyloric plane.

Fig. xiv, 27.

The *inferior mesenteric* (level of the 3rd lumbar vertebra) arises from the left side of the main trunk at about the level of the subcostal plane.

Fig. xiv, 28.

The *common iliac artery* corresponds to the upper third of a line drawn from a point ½ inch below and to the left of the umbilicus to a second point situated half-way between the anterior superior iliac spine and the pubic symphysis. The *external iliac* artery corresponds in direction to the lower two-thirds of this line.

Fig. xiv, 29.

Fig. xiv, 31.

The *inferior epigastric artery* is given off from the external iliac just as that vessel passes under the inguinal ligament half-way between the anterior superior iliac spine and the pubic symphysis. The epigastric artery then passes upwards and inwards along the medial side of the deep inguinal ring towards a point immediately external to the umbilicus, entering the rectus sheath at the level of the arcuate line.

Fig. xx, 20.

This vessel forms the lateral boundary of *the inguinal*

triangle (of Hesselbach), the medial boundary being
formed by the linea semilunaris of the same
side, and the base by the inguinal ligament.
Each triangle is subdivided in a vertical direction into
two parts by the obliterated umbilical artery, on either
side of which herniæ may protrude.

Fig. xx, 16.

The *inferior vena cava* is formed by the junction of the
two common iliac veins on the right side of the body of
the 5th lumbar vertebra, about 1 inch below and ½ inch
to the right of the umbilicus. The vein passes upwards
through the venacaval opening of the diaphragm at the level of the 8th thoracic
vertebra, entering the right auricle of the heart opposite
the 5th right interspace and the adjoining part of the
sternum.

Fig. xiv, 23.

THE LIVER.

The anterior border can be mapped out by drawing a
curved line from a point in the 5th left interspace 3½ inches from the middle line (the
position of the apex of the heart), the line cutting the
left costal margin at the tip of the 8th costal cartilage
and the right costal margin at the tip of the 9th costal
cartilage. Between these two latter points, the anterior
border of the liver crosses the middle line half-way
between the umbilicus and the xiphisternal joint (= transpyloric plane), whilst a notch to the right of the middle
line indicates the hepatic attachment of the
ligamentum teres, which passes from that
notch downwards and inwards to the umbilicus.

Fig. xx, 2.

Fig. xx, 4.

Beyond the tip of the 9th right costal cartilage the
anterior border of the liver follows the lower
limit of the costal arch, descending sometimes

Fig. xvi, 12.

even below that level, and after cutting across the 12th rib, ascends towards the level of the 11th thoracic spine.

The *upper limit of the liver* is indicated by a line starting as before in the 5th left interspace 3½ inches from the middle line, and ascending slightly as it passes to the right. This line cuts across the 6th right chondro-sternal articulation, the upper border of the right 5th costal cartilage in the right lateral vertical plane, the 6th rib in the mid-axillary line, sweeping thence just below the angle of the scapula towards the 8th thoracic spine.

Fig. xx.

The *gall-bladder.*—The fundus projects from under the anterior border of the liver in the angle between the tips of the 9th and 10th costal cartilages and the outer border of the rectus abdominis muscle.

Fig. xx, 3.

The *diaphragm.*—On ordinary inspiration the right dome of the diaphragm corresponds in level to the lower part of the 4th right interspace, whilst the left dome ascends to the lower part of the 5th left rib and costal cartilage.

Fig. xx, 1.

The Common Bile-Duct, etc.

The *lesser omentum*, passing upwards from the lesser curvature of the stomach to the porta hepatis of the liver, presents a free edge, which looks downwards and to the right, and which forms the anterior boundary of the *aditus to the lesser sac* (foramen of Winslow)—the channel of communication between the greater and the lesser peritoneal sacs. The free edge of this omentum contains (between its two layers of peritoneum) three important structures :

Fig. xix, 16.

Fig. xix, 17.

1. The common bile-duct to the right.
2. The hepatic artery to the left.

FIG. XX.

1, 1. The diaphragm.
2. The liver.
3. The gall-bladder.
4. The ligamentum teres
5. The cisterna chyli.
6. The thoracic duct.
7. The venous termination of the duct.
8. The internal mammary artery.
9. The superior epigastric artery.
10. The musculo-phrenic artery.
11. The rectus abdominis muscle.
12, 12. The lineæ semilunares.
13, 13, 13. The lineæ transversæ.
14. The arcuate line (semilunar fold of Douglas).
15. The urachus.
16. The inguinal triangle (Hesselbach).
17, 17. The deep inguinal ring.
18, 18. The superficial inguinal ring.
19, 19. The inguinal canal.
20. The inferior epigastric artery.

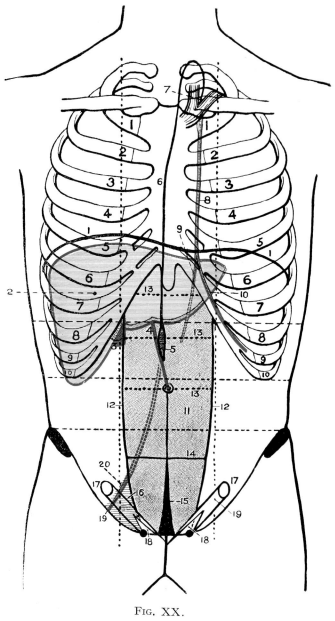

FIG. XX.

To face p. 64.

3. The portal vein behind and between the two former structures.

In mapping out any of these structures, it is, therefore, advisable first to draw in the lesser curvature of the stomach, the pylorus, the three parts of the duodenum, and the pancreas. The pylorus occupies such a definite position in the transpyloric plane that all these structures are easily and quickly drawn in. The free margin of the lesser omentum should be represented as a curved line passing upwards and to the right for $1\frac{1}{2}$ to 2 inches from the duodeno-pyloric junction. The *portal vein* is formed behind the head of the pancreas by the union of the superior mesenteric and splenic veins, and passes upwards to the porta hepatis of the liver behind the first part of the duodenum, and in the free edge of the lesser omentum.

The *hepatic artery*, a branch of the cœliac artery, passes upwards from the upper border of the first part of the duodenum, in the free edge of the lesser omentum, to the porta hepatis.

The *common bile-duct* is 3 inches long, and is formed
Fig. xix, 18. by the union of the common hepatic and cystic ducts. It passes downwards in the free edge of the lesser omentum, behind the first part of the duodenum behind the head of the pancreas, and opens on the inner and posterior aspect of the second or descending part of the duodenum.

THE SPLEEN.

The long axis of the spleen corresponds to the 10th
Fig. xvi, 9. rib, and the viscus extends upwards to the upper border of the 9th rib, and downwards to the lower border of the 11th rib. The upper and inner pole lies $1\frac{1}{2}$ to 2 inches away from the 10th thoracic spine,

whilst the lower or anterior pole reaches as far forwards as the mid-axillary line.

THE SPINAL CORD.

The spinal cord extends from the foramen magnum to Fig. vii, 5. the lower border of the 1st lumbar vertebra Fig. xvi, 2. (transpyloric plane). The cord follows the curves of the vertebral column, and presents also two enlargements, cervical and lumbar. The former swelling lies between the 3rd cervical and 2nd thoracic vertebræ, the latter between the 9th and 12th thoracic vertebræ. Near its termination the cord tapers away as the *conus medullaris*.

The *filum terminale*, the prolongation of the cord, is Fig. vii, 7. continued onwards from the lower part of the Fig. xvi, 3. body of the 1st lumbar vertebra to near the tip of the coccyx, at which level it blends with the periosteum lining that bone.

The spinal dural sheath, extends as low as the 3rd Fig. vii, 6. sacral vertebra, at which level it is pierced by Fig. xvi, 1, 1. the filum terminale.

A line uniting the two posterior superior iliac spines Fig. vii, 10. cuts across the 2nd sacral spine, and the dural Fig. xvi, 15. sac, therefore, terminates about ½ inch below the level of this interspinous line. At the third month of intra-uterine life the cord extends the whole length of the vertebral canal, whilst at birth it reaches as low down as the 3rd lumbar vertebra.

A reference to Fig. 7 will show that cerebro-spinal fluid might be withdrawn from the dural canal anywhere between the termination of the cord at the level of the transpyloric plane and the base of the sacrum. A line drawn across the back, at right angles to the long axis of the body, at the level of the highest part of the iliac crests, cuts across the middle line of the back at the level of the interspace between the laminæ of the 3rd and 4th vertebræ. It is at this point, or rather to one side of this point, that *lumbar puncture* is carried out.

THE PERINEUM.

A brief account only will be given, as, though the landmarks are most important, the tendency is great to drift into the question of surgical applied anatomy—a pitfall which the writer is most anxious to avoid.

The *perineum* is, in shape, roughly quadrilateral, the lateral boundaries being formed in front by the diverging rami of the pubis and ischium, and behind by the ischial tuberosity and the gluteus maximus muscle. The anterior and posterior angles of the space are formed respectively by the pubic symphysis and the tip of the coccyx. The pubic arch angle is obtuse in the female and acute in the male. In the female, also, the ischial tuberosities are further apart and slightly everted. The *perineum* is divided into two areas by a line drawn between the anterior part of the ischial tuberosities, thus forming—

(*a*) The urogenital area.
(*b*) The anal area.

This transverse line passes about 1 inch in front of the anus, and represents the level of the two transversus perinei superficialis muscles, the posterior border of the perineal membrane (triangular ligament), and the line along which the membranous layer of the superficial fascia (Colles's fascia), is reflected round the posterior border of the two transverse perinei muscles to become continuous with the posterior border of the perineal membrane. The " *central tendinous point of the perineum* "

6

(perineal body), corresponds to the middle of this line, and forms the point of attachment of several muscles.

(a) The *urogenital area.*—In the *male* this area is divided into two lateral triangles by the median antero-posterior prominence of the bulb of the penis (corpus spongiosum). The two crura of the penis (corpora cavernosa) diverge as they pass backwards towards the tuberosity of the ischium, and the main pudendal vessels lie under cover of these erectile organs. The triangle is completed behind by the transversus perinei muscle. All the above-mentioned erectile structures and muscles lie superficial to the perineal membrane.

In the *female*, this area is practically cut into two lateral triangles, by the orifice of the vagina, each side of which lies the bulb of the vestibule, an organ of erectile tissue, corresponding developmentally to the male corpus spongiosum. More superficially, the two labia majora converge towards the mons pubis in front, whilst, on the inner aspect of the labia majora, the labia minora converge towards the clitoris, between which body and the vaginal margin a smooth triangular space exists—the *vestibule.* At the junction of the vagina and the vestibule the *urethra* opens.

Vaginal examination.—Passing along the posterior vaginal wall the finger enters the posterior fornix, the upper part of which is in *direct relation with the peritoneal cavity* (Douglas's pouch). Along the anterior wall the smaller anterior fornix is first encountered, this *cul-de-sac* not being directly related to the peritoneal cavity, and immediately above this the *cervix uteri* may be examined. Bimanually, much information can usually be gained with regard to the size and position of the uterus, the condition of the uterine appendages, the contents of Douglas's pouch, etc.

(b) *The anal area.*—This area is divided into two lateral parts by a line drawn from the " central point of the perineum " to the tip of the coccyx, and the examining fingers may, in thin subjects, be made to sink deeply into each lateral recess (the ischiorectal fossæ), being then in relation with the rectum and levator ani muscle on the inner side, the ischial tuberosity and the obturator internus muscle on the outer side, the transverse perinei muscle in front, and the gluteus maximus and sacro-tuberous ligament behind.

Rectal examination.—If the forefinger be gently inserted into the rectum, definite resistance is offered by the external and internal sphincters, the latter aided by contraction of the levator ani muscle. Further on the finger enters the dilated ampullary portion of the rectum, meeting, perhaps, further obstruction from the transverse rectal folds (valves of Houston). When insinuated as far as possible, the palmar aspect of the distal phalanx will, in the male, be in contact with the vasa deferentia, the vesiculæ seminales and the base of the bladder, the middle phalanx with the prostate gland, and the proximal phalanx with the sphincters, which intervene between the finger and the perineal membrane and the spongy and membranous parts of the urethra. Posteriorly, the hollow of the sacrum and the coccyx can be explored. It is most important to bear in mind that the peritoneum is reflected from the rectum on to the *upper third of the vagina in the female, and on to the vesiculæ seminales, about* 1 *inch above the upper limit of the prostate gland, in the male.*

In *children,* since the true pelvis is but little developed and the later pelvic viscera are practically abdominal, a rectal examination enables one to explore all the lower abdominal viscera, including the bladder.

In the *female,* the cervix uteri can be felt, projecting against the anterior rectal wall.

CHAPTER V

THE LOWER LIMB

THE pubic tubercle, the iliac crest, the anterior and posterior superior iliac spines and the iliac tubercles have all been alluded to previously and located. It has also been stated that a line uniting the two posterior superior iliac spines cuts across the spine of the 2nd sacral vertebra. Below this line the remaining sacral spines and the coccyx are easily felt, though the coccyx itself is more readily verified by inserting the forefinger into the rectum whilst the thumb is placed over the bone externally.

Fig. xxi.

The region of the hip.—(*a*) Posterior and lateral aspect : The greater trochanter of the femur and the ischial tuberosity must now be examined. The latter process lies under cover of the lower part of the gluteus maximus muscle, whilst the trochanter is subcutaneous in its lower part, and covered over in front and above by the insertion of the gluteus medius muscle.

The trochanter is more or less quadrilateral in shape, fading off into the shaft of the femur below, and presenting a well-marked posterior border; the highest point of the trochanter corresponds to the posterior superior angle of the quadrilateral. When the body is in the erect position, there is a well-defined depression, situated above and behind the great trochanter, which becomes less marked when, as the result of disease

Fig. xxi, 2.
Fig. xxiv, 6.

FIG. XXI.

1. Posterior superior iliac spine.
2. Greater trochanter of femur.
3. Nélaton's line, from ischial tuberosity to the anterior superior iliac spine, cutting across the summit of the greater trochanter.
4. Piriformis muscle.
5. Sciatic nerve.
6. Medial popliteal nerve.
7. Lateral popliteal nerve.
8. Posterior tibial nerve.
9. Popliteal space.
10. Biceps tendon.
11. Semimembranosus and semitendinosus.
12. Plantaris and lateral head of gastrocnemius.
13. Medial head of gastrocnemius.
14. The short saphenous vein.

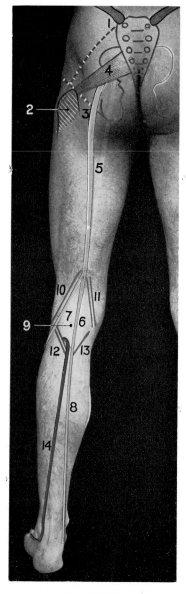

FIG. XXI.

To face p. 70.

or disuse, **the** gluteus maximus undergoes atrophic changes. The fold of the nates does not correspond to the lower border of the gluteus maximus muscle, as it crosses almost transversely the lower oblique fibres of that muscle. This fold also becomes less distinct when the glutei muscles degenerate. The head and neck of the femur form with the shaft of that bone an angle of 125 *to* 130 *degrees*.

Fig. xxi.

Nélaton's line.—" If in the normal state you examine the relation of the greater trochanter to the other bony prominences of the pelvis, you will find that the top of the greater trochanter corresponds to a line drawn from the anterior superior iliac spine of the ilium to the most prominent point of the tuberosity of the ischium. This line also runs through the centre of the acetabulum. The extent of displacement in dislocation or in fracture is marked by the projection of the trochanter behind and above this line " (Nélaton).

Fig. xxi, 3.
Fig. xxiv, 5.

Bryant's triangle.—When the patient is in the dorsal recumbent position, draw a line round the body at the level of the anterior superior iliac spine, and from this line drop a perpendicular to the top of the great trochanter. To complete the triangle, draw a line from the anterior superior iliac spine to the top of the trochanter. When the trochanter is displaced upwards the perpendicular line is diminished in length as compared with the sound side, and when it undergoes a backward displacement the spino-trochanteric line is relatively increased in length.

Fig. xxiv, 4.

(*b*)—Anterior and medial aspect : The lower limb is demarcated from the abdomen by a well-marked furrow, the *inguinal groove*. This corresponds to the situation of the inguinal ligament (*Poupart's ligament*), the recurved

lower border of the obliquus externus abdominis muscle.
This ligament, as it passes from the anterior superior
iliac spine to the pubic tubercle of the same side, forms the
upper boundary of the *femoral triangle* (Scarpa's triangle),
a space which is best demonstrated when the thigh is

Figs. xxii, xxiii. flexed, abducted, and everted. The sartorius
muscle is then thrown into action and the
outer boundary of the space so shown. If the hand be now
placed on the upper and inner aspect of the thigh and the
limb be sharply adducted, a rounded tendon at once
becomes noticeable. This is the adductor longus, which
forms the inner boundary of the femoral triangle.

The outwardly directed adductor longus and the
inwardly curving sartorius converge to form the apex of
the triangle.

The floor of the space is formed from without inwards
by the iliacus, psoas major, pectineus and adductor longus
muscles. In the superficial fascia which overlies this
region numerous lymphatic glands are situated, and it
will here be convenient to discuss briefly their general
arrangement. The *superficial lymphatic glands* are placed
in three main groups :

(1) The *oblique or inguinal* glands, running parallel to
and below the inguinal ligament, and draining the anterior
aspect of the abdomen below the level of the umbilicus,
the lower half of the side and back, the gluteal region,
and the upper and outer part of the thigh.

(2) The *vertical or femoral* glands, running with the long
saphenous vein, and draining the greater part of the inner
aspect of the foot, leg, and thigh.

(3) The *pubic* glands, situated below and lateral to the
pubic tubercle, and draining mainly the external genitals,
perineum, and anus.

FIG. XXII.

1. The anterior superior iliac spine.
2. The pubic tubercle.
3. The inguinal ligament (Poupart's ligament).
4. The sartorius muscle.
5. The adductor longus muscle.
6. The femoral nerve.
7. Femoral arteries.
8. Femoral vein.
9. Femoral ring.
10. Saphenous vein and opening.
11. Upper limit of knee-joint (subcrureus pouch)
12. Level of knee-joint.
13. The long saphenous vein.
14. Anterior tibial artery.
15. Anterior tibial nerve.

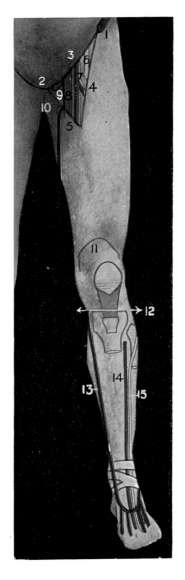

FIG. XXII.

To face p. 72.

The deep fascia presents an opening, the *saphenous*
opening, for the transmission of the long
saphenous vein to the femoral vein. This foramen is oval in shape, being 1 inch long and
½ to ¾ inch broad, the long axis vertical. The central
point of the opening is situated 1½ *inches below and* 1½
inches lateral to the pubic tubercle.

Fig. xxii,
10.
Fig. xxiii,
13.

Beneath the deep fascia overlying the femoral triangle
certain important structures are situated, such as the
femoral artery, superficial branches, and profunda
femoris arteries, the corresponding veins, and the femoral
nerve. These will all be dealt with later, the femoral
ring alone needing here further definition.

The *femoral ring*, through which a femoral hernia commonly escapes from the abdominal cavity, lies
below the medial part of the inguinal ligament,
and lateral to the pubic tubercle. A good way
to define the ring with precision is that recommended by
Holden : " Feel for the pulsation of the (common) femoral
artery, allow ½ inch on the inner side for the femoral
vein, then comes the femoral ring." The femoral ring
presents the following boundaries : To the inner side is
Gimbernat's ligament* ; to the lateral side is the femoral
vein ; in front is the inguinal ligament ; behind is the
pectineus muscle and the horizontal ramus of the os pubis.

Fig. xxii,
9.
Fig. xxiii,
7.

The *subsartorial canal* (Hunter's canal), a more or less
triangular muscular channel for the transmission of the femoral artery, occupies the
middle third of the antero-medial aspect of the thigh.
During forcible contraction of the thigh muscles, the
femoral triangle may be seen to be continued downwards
as a shallow depression between the extensor and adductor

Fig. xxiii,
10.

* This is the lacunar ligament, the pectineal reflection of the
inguinal ligament.

muscles, this furrow corresponding to the position of the canal in question. The anatomical boundaries of the canal are (1) vastus medialis laterally, (2) adductor posterior longus and magnus posterior, (3) sartorius and a strong fascial band between the adductors and vastus medialis in front and medially.

The canal transmits the femoral vein and artery, the saphenous nerve and the nerve to the vastus medialis.

In order to *compare the length* of the lower extremities the limbs should be placed parallel to one another, and the tape-measure carried from the anterior superior iliac spine to the tip of the medial malleolus of the tibia of the same side. The distance between these two points may be subdivided, if necessary, by marking out, on the medial aspect of the knee, the transverse line which indicates the level of the knee-joint. The lengths of the femur and of the tibia are thus separately estimated.

Fig. xxii, 12.

The *region of the knee.*—The biceps tendon forms the upper and lateral boundary of the popliteal space, and under cover of this tendon, on its medial or popliteal aspect, a cord-like structure is felt, the *lateral popliteal nerve.* This intimate relation of tendon and of nerve must be remembered in the operation of tenotomy of the biceps tendon. If the biceps tendon be now traced downwards the head of the fibula is reached, this process lying below, lateral, and on a posterior plane to the lateral tuberosity of the tibia. The styloid process of the head of the fibula projects upwards from the posterior part of the head, and in front of this the rounded long lateral ligament of the knee-joint can be traced upwards to its femoral attachment. In front of

Fig. xxi, 9.

Fig. xxi, 7, 10.

Fig. xxiii, 1, 3.

FIG. XXIII.

Right leg.

1. Biceps tendon.
2. Ilio-tibial tract.
3. Lateral popliteal nerve.
4. Anterior tibial nerve.
5. Musculo-cutaneous nerve.
6. Anterior tibial artery.
7. The short saphenous vein.

Left leg.

1. Anterior superior iliac spine.
2. Pubic tubercle.
3. The inguinal ligament.
4. The femoral nerve.
5. The femoral artery.
6. The femoral vein.
7. Femoral ring.
8. The femoral artery, below profunda branch.
9. Profunda femoris artery.
10. The subsartorial canal (Hunter's canal), between the two upper arrows.
11. Arrow indicating the position of the adductor tubercle and the lower femoral epiphyseal line.
12. The long saphenous vein.
13. Saphenous opening.

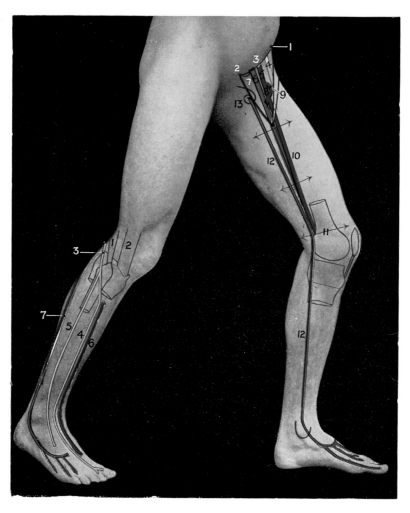

Fig. XXIII.

To face p. 74.

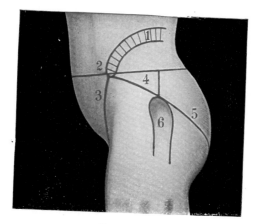

FIG. XXIV.

1. Iliac crest.
2. Anterior superior iliac spine.
3. The inguinal ligament.
4. Bryant's triangle.
5. Nélaton's line.
6. Great trochanter of femur.

To follow Fig. XXIII.

the biceps tendon there is a depression which is bounded
Fig. xxiii, anteriorly by the broad iliotibial tract. Two
2. well-marked tendons bound the popliteal space
on the upper and medial side, the semimembranosus and
semitendinosus. The latter is the more lateral, the
Fig. xxi, more superficial, and the narrower, and the
11. long rounded tendon can be traced some
distance up into the thigh. The semimembranosus
tendon lies to the inner side of the semitendinosus and
on a deeper plane. The broad tendon can be traced
downwards to its insertion into the inner and posterior
aspect of the medial tuberosity of the tibia. On the
inner aspect of the knee the tendon of the gracilis muscle
and the lower part of the sartorius muscle form a fairly
well-marked prominence, the individual muscles being,
however, usually incapable of clear definition owing to
their flattened shape. Between these tendons and the
prominent vastus medialis muscle a depression exists, and
by deep palpation the adductor magnus tendon may be
felt lying under cover of the inner margin of the vastus
medialis muscle. By tracing this tendon downwards to
Fig. xxiii, its insertion the *adductor tubercle* is reached.
11. This tubercle corresponds also to the level of
the *lower epiphyseal line* of the femur.

The sartorius and gracilis muscles, though not easily
defined on the inner side of the knee, form, together
with the semitendinosus muscle, a fairly well-
Fig. xxiii. marked elevation below the medial tuberosity
of the tibia, which is directed downwards, forwards, and
outwards.

The *ligamentum patellæ* narrows off as it passes from
the inferior border of the patella to the tibial
Fig. xxii. tubercle, and on each side of the ligament

depressions exist, in the lower part of which the medial and lateral tuberosities of the tibia are readily felt.

The *prepatellar bursa* extends from the middle of the patella to the tibial tubercle. Laterally, the bursa falls just short of the patellar border.

The *synovial membrane* of the knee-joint extends up-
Fig. xxii, wards about three fingers' breadth above the
11. upper border of the patella when the leg is in the extended position, reaching up under the vastus medialis to a slightly higher level than on the other side. Laterally, the synovial membrane extends to near the medial and lateral margins of the femoral condyles, whilst the lower limit is situated just above the tubercle of the tibia. When the joint is distended with fluid the outline of the joint cavity becomes marked, and the depressions which normally exist each side of the patellar ligament become obliterated.

The *ankle and foot*.—The lateral malleolus projects
Fig. xxvi, about $\frac{1}{2}$ inch below the medial, and also lies
1, 2. on a more posterior plane. The ankle-joint corresponds in level to a point about $\frac{1}{2}$ inch above the tip of the medial malleolus.

About 1 inch below and $\frac{1}{2}$ inch in front of the terminal process of the lateral malleolus is the *peroneal tubercle*,
Fig. xxv, which separates the peroneus brevis above
3. from the longus below. The two peronei
Fig. xxviii, tendons, when traced upwards, are found to
4. pass behind the lateral malleolus. About 1 inch in front of the peroneal tubercle is the prominent tubercle of
the base of the fifth metatarsal bone, to which
Fig. xxv. the peroneus brevis is attached. Between the peroneal tubercle and the base of the fifth metatarsal bone the cuboid bone may be felt, grooved on its outer and

FIG. XXV

Right foot.

1. Peroneus longus
2. Peroneus brevis.
3. Peroneal tubercle of calcaneum.
4. Head of calcaneum and origin of the extensor digitorum brevis muscle.
5. Peroneus tertius.
6. Extensor digitorum longus.
7. Innermost tendon of extensor digitorum longus.

Left foot.

1. Tibialis posterior.
2. Flexor digitorum longus (passing over sustentaculum tali).
3. Flexor hallucis longus.
4. Tendo calcaneus (Achilles).
5. Sustentaculum tali (of calcaneum).
6. Tuberosity of the navicular.
7. Head of talus.
8. Tibialis anterior.
9. Extensor hallucis longus.

THE REGION OF THE ANKLE AND FOOT

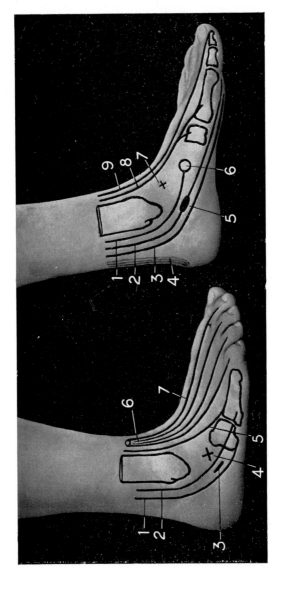

Fig. XXV.

under aspect by the peroneus longus tendon. The tendon crosses the plantar aspect of the foot in a forward and inward direction, to be inserted into the lateral aspect of the base of the first metatarsal bone. Immediately in **Fig. xxv,** front of the lateral malleolus there is a well-**4.** marked depression, which is bounded in front by a prominence due to the fleshy mass of the extensor digitorum brevis, and above by the tendon of the peroneus tertius.

If the floor of this depression be examined, the head of the talus will be felt above and to the medial side, and the head of the calcaneum below and to the lateral side.

Between the two malleoli in front of the ankle-joint four tendons can be felt. The most prominent and the **Fig. xxv.** innermost is the tendon of the tibialis anterior muscle. Lateral to this follow the extensor hallucis longus, the extensor digitorum longus, and the peroneus tertius. When the foot is well extended, the head of the talus can also be identified lying under cover of the extensor tendons.

Fig. xxv, Immediately below the medial malleolus is **5.** the *sustentaculum tali*, grooved on its under **Fig. xxv,** **2.** aspect by the flexor hallucis longus tendon.

The tibialis posterior tendon can be traced upwards **Fig. xxv,** behind the medial malleolus and downwards to **6.** the tuberosity of the navicular bone, to which process the tendon gains its main attachment. In front of the medial malleolus there is another depression, which lies below the line of the tibialis anterior tendon, and here the head of the talus can again be felt, especially pro-**Fig. xxv,** minent when the foot is well everted. About **7.** 1 inch below and in front of the medial mal-**Fig. xxv,** **6.** leolus the tuberosity of the navicular bon forms the most prominent bony point on the medial side of the foot, and a line which joins the tip of the medial

Fig. xxv. malleolus, the head of the talus, and the navicular tubercle, normally presents a slight upward convexity.

In flat-foot, the head of the talus undergoes a downward displacement, and the line uniting the three bony points becomes straight, or even downwardly convex.

A line drawn almost transversely across the foot from a point proximal to the navicular tuberosity indicates the level of the *transverse tarsal joint*.

Fig. xxv. In front of the navicular tuberosity, the medial cuneiform and the first metatarsal bones may be located and verified.

Behind the ankle-joint the tendo calcaneus (Achilles) is

Fig. xxv,
4. placed, the tendon being at its narrowest at a point about $1\frac{1}{2}$ inches above its insertion into the posterior part of the calcaneum. When distended with fluid, the synovial membrane of the ankle-joint bulges outwards, so as to obliterate the depressions that normally lie between the tendo calcaneus and the two malleoli.

The *extensor retinacular ligaments of the ankle.*—The

Fig. xxvi,
3. superior portion of this ligament, about 1 inch broad, extends transversely across the ankle from tibia to fibula. It presents two compartments only,

Fig. xxvi,
6. one for the tibialis anterior, and one for the remaining extensor tendons. The former tendon alone possesses a synovial sheath.

The inferior portion of the ligament is Y-shaped, the

Fig. xxvi,
4. single limb arising from the upper and lateral aspect of the head of the calcaneum in close connection with the origin of the extensor digitorum brevis muscle. The upper limb of the divided portion

THE REGION OF THE ANKLE AND FOOT

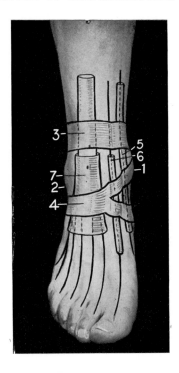

Fig. XXVI.

1. The medial malleolus.
2. The lateral malleolus.
3. The superior transverse band of the extensor retinaculum.
4. The Y-shaped inferior portion of the extensor retinaculum.
5. The tibialis anterior synovial sheath.
6. The extensor hallucis longus synovial sheath.
7. The extensor digitorum longus and peroneus tertius synovial sheath.

To face p. 78.

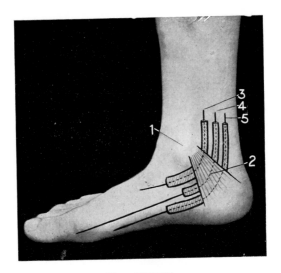

Fig. XXVII.

1. The medial malleolus.
2. The flexor retinaculum.
3. The tibialis posterior synovial sheath.
4. The flexor digitorum longus synovial sheath.
5. The flexor hallucis longus synovial sheath.

To face p. 79.

becomes attached to the medial malleolus, whilst the lower limb sweeps over to the navicular tuberosity and to the medial side of the foot. The extensor digitorum **Fig. xxvi, 7.** longus and the peroneus tertius pass under the single undivided limb, and possess in this situation a common synovial sheath ; whilst the extensor **Fig. xxvi, 5, 6.** hallucis longus and the tibialis anterior pass through separate compartments in each limb of the divided portion of the ligament, and each tendon in so doing is surrounded by a synovial sheath, that enveloping the tibialis anterior tendon being continuous with the sheath already alluded to as enclosing the tendon under the transverse portion of the ligament.

The *flexor retinaculum* is triangular in shape, the **Fig. xxvii, 2.** apex being attached to the medial malleolus, and the base to the lower margin of the calcaneum. From the deep aspect of the ligament septa are given off which form separate compartments for the **Fig. xxvii, 3, 4, 5.** passage of the tendons of the tibialis posterior, flexor digitorum longus, and flexor hallucis longus muscles, each tendon having its own synovial sheath. These three sheaths extend for about 1 inch above the upper limit of the retinacular ligament ; and although the sheath enveloping the tibialis posterior reaches almost as far forwards as the navicular tuberosity, the other two sheaths usually terminate about ½ inch **Fig. xxix, 2, 3.** below the inferior margin of the ligament. The flexor hallucis longus and flexor digitorum longus have, again, distinct synovial sheaths just before their insertion into the distal phalanges of the toes, these sheaths, however, being very variable, and rarely extending further backwards than the heads of the metatarsal bones.

The *peroneal retinaculum* is less definite in shape and can only be described as a broad band passing from the lateral malleolus to the lower margin of the calcaneum.

Fig. xxviii, 1, 2, 3, 4.   Beneath it two tendons pass—the peroneus longus and brevis. These two tendons possess a common synovial sheath, which extends upwards 2 to 3 inches above the tip of the lateral malleolus, and downwards as far as the peroneal tubercle, where the sac divides into two, one part accompanying the peroneus brevis to near the base of the fifth metatarsal bone, the other extending forwards to the outer and under aspect of the cuboid bone. The

Fig. xxix, 1, 4.   peroneus longus is also usually enclosed in a synovial sheath in the last inch or so of its course, previous to its insertion into the lateral aspect of the base of the first metatarsal bone.

The Vessels and Nerves of the Lower Limb.

The *superior gluteal artery* emerges from the greater

Fig. xxi.   sciatic foramen, above the piriformis muscle, at the junction of the inner and middle thirds of a line drawn from the posterior superior iliac spine to the top of the greater trochanter of the femur of the same side.

The *inferior gluteal artery* may be ligatured at a point

Fig. xxi.   which lies just lateral to the junction of the middle and lower thirds of a line drawn from the posterior superior iliac spine to the outer part of the ischial tuberosity of the same side. This line also cuts across the *posterior inferior iliac spine* and the tip of the *ischial spine*, whilst the *internal pudendal artery* lies immediately medial to the seat of election for ligation of the inferior gluteal artery.

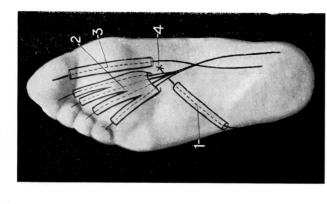

FIG. XXIX.

1. The peroneus longus synovial sheath.
2. The flexor digitorum longus synovial sheath.
3. The flexor hallucis longus synovial sheath.
4. The insertion of peroneus longus into base of 1st metatarsal bone.

To face p. 80.

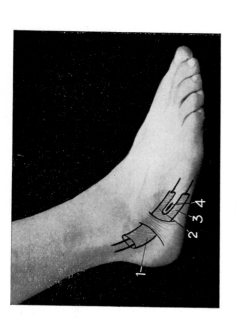

FIG. XXVIII.

1. The peroneus longus and brevis synovial sheath.
2. The peroneus brevis sheath.
3. The peroneus longus sheath.
4. The peroneal tubercle.

The *femoral artery*.—With the thigh flexed, everted,
Figs. xxii and xxiii. and slightly abducted, this vessel corresponds in direction to a line drawn from a point midway between the anterior superior iliac spine and the pubic symphysis to the adductor tubercle of the femur below.

Fig. xxiii, 5. The upper 1½ inches of this line = the femoral artery, before the profunda femoris is given off.

Fig. xxii, 7. The upper third = the femoral artery in the femoral triangle.

The upper two-thirds = the complete course of the femoral artery.

Fig. xxiii, 10. The middle third = the femoral artery in the subsartorial canal.

The *popliteal artery* enters the upper angle of the popliteal space (from the medial side) by passing between the femur and the adductor magnus tendon. The vessel at first passes obliquely outwards and downwards to the mid-point of the space, and then changes direction by passing vertically downwards as far as the lower border of the popliteus muscle, at which level it bifurcates into anterior and posterior tibial arteries. The point of bifurcation corresponds to the level of the tubercle of the tibia.

The *anterior tibial artery*.—The course of this vessel
Fig. xxii, 14. Fig. xxiii, 6. may be indicated by a line drawn from a point just below the level of the tibial tubercle, and midway between the lateral tuberosity of the tibia and the head of the fibula, to a second point in front of the ankle midway between the two malleoli, at which level the artery lies between the tendons of the extensor hallucis longus and digitorum longus muscles.

The anterior tibial artery is continued onwards as the *dorsalis pedis* as far as the base of the first interosseous space.

The *posterior tibial artery* starts at the lower border of the popliteus muscle as one of the terminal branches of the popliteal artery. It can be represented by a line which starts at the inferior angle of the popliteal space, on a level with the tubercle of the tibia, and which passes downwards and inwards to the mid-point between the posterior border of the medial malleolus and the medial border of the calcaneum. At this level it lies under cover of the flexor retinaculum, and bifurcates in this situation into the medial and lateral plantar arteries Behind the medial malleolus the posterior tibial artery lies between the tendons of the flexor hallucis longus and digitorum longus muscles, but on a slightly superficial plane.

The *medial plantar artery* passes forwards to the

Fig. xxix.

cleft between the first and second toes, whilst the more important *lateral plantar artery* is first directed forwards and outwards towards the base of the fifth metatarsal bone, and then, changing direction,

Fig. xxix.

passes forwards and inwards to the base of the first interosseous space, forming in this latter part of its course the *plantar arch*. It anastomoses with the dorsalis pedis artery, which dips downwards between the two heads of the first dorsal interosseous muscle.

The *short saphenous vein* arises from the lateral side of

Fig. xxi, 14.
Fig. xxiii, 7.

the venous arch on the dorsum of the foot, passing upwards behind the lateral malleolus and along the lateral and posterior part of the leg to the middle of the popliteal space, where it pierces the deep fascia to open into the popliteal vein. It is accompanied in the greater part of its course by the *sural nerve*, which extends forwards on the lateral side of the foot as far as the tip of the little toe.

The *long saphenous vein* arises from the inner side of the venous arch found on the dorsum of the foot. It passes upwards in front of the medial malleolus, along the inner side of the leg and knee, behind the medial condyle of the femur, and its further upward course in the thigh is indicated by a line drawn from the adductor tubercle to the saphenous opening. Attention has previously been drawn to the elevation below the medial tuberosity of the tibia which is formed by the sartorius, gracilis and semitendinosus muscles, and below this prominence the saphenous vein is accompanied by the *saphenous nerve*, a branch of the deep division of the femoral nerve. The saphenous nerve runs down the leg with the vein, in front of the medial malleolus of the tibia, and extends as far forwards as the ball of the great toe. In the thigh the nerve crosses in front of the femoral artery from without inwards, and accompanies that artery throughout the whole length of the subsartorial canal.

Fig. xxii, 13.
Fig. xxiii, 12.

The *femoral nerve* emerges from under cover of the inguinal ligament, about half-way between the anterior superior iliac spine and the pubic tubercle. The nerve lies nearly $\frac{1}{2}$ inch lateral to the femoral artery, and the same distance lateral to the femoral sheath.

Fig. xxii, 6.
Fig. xxiii, 4.

The *sciatic nerve* makes its exit from the pelvis through the greater sciatic foramen below the piriformis muscle. The nerve emerges from under cover of the lower border of the gluteus maximus muscle just to the medial side of the mid-point between

Fig. xxi, 5.

the ischial tuberosity and the greater trochanter of the femur. The nerve corresponds in direction to the upper two-thirds of a line drawn downwards from the above point to the middle of the popliteal space below. At the junction of the middle and lower thirds of the thigh the sciatic nerve divides into its two terminal branches—medial and lateral popliteal.

The *posterior femoral cutaneous* (*small sciatic*) *nerve* lies in the same line as the sciatic, but extends downwards as far as the inferior angle of the popliteal space.

The *medial popliteal nerve* crosses the popliteal artery superficially from without inwards; its onward continuation, the *posterior tibial nerve*, and the two terminal branches of the posterior tibial nerve, the *medial and lateral plantars*, all have the same surface marking as the corresponding arteries. Two points, however, need to be borne in mind : first, the posterior tibial nerve crosses the corresponding artery superficially from within outwards and downwards, and, secondly, the medial plantar nerve is relatively much more important than the corresponding artery.

Fig. xxi, 6, 8.

The *lateral popliteal nerve* was last seen to lie under cover of the biceps femoris tendon at the upper and lateral boundary of the popliteal space. The nerve follows the tendon downwards to the head of the fibula, and curls round to the antero-lateral aspect of the leg about 1 inch below the head of that bone, dividing there into its two terminal branches, anterior tibial and musculocutaneous.

Fig. xxi, 7.

The *anterior tibial nerve* passes downwards and inwards to join the corresponding artery, lying lateral to the upper third of the artery, superficial to the middle third, and lateral again to the lower

Fig. xxii, 15.

third. The nerve extends forwards along the lateral side of the dorsalis pedis artery as far as the cleft between the first and second toes, the contiguous sides of which toes it supplies.

The *musculocutaneous nerve,* running down in the sub-
stance of the peronei muscles, becomes cuta-neous below the middle of the leg. It then passes obliquely downwards and inwards across the extensor retinaculum, to be distributed to the greater part of the dorsal surface of the foot.

APPENDIX

THE LENGTH OF VARIOUS PASSAGES, TUBES, ETC.

THE spinal cord, 16 to 18 inches.

The trachea, 4½ inches.

The right bronchus, 1 inch.

The left bronchus, 1½ to 2 inches.

The pharynx, 4½ inches.

The œsophagus, 9 to 10 inches.*

The stomach :

      Capacity, about 2 pints.

      Length, 10 inches.

      Width, 4 to 5 inches.

Duodenum, 8 to 10 inches.

Bile-duct, 3 inches.

Small intestine, 23 feet.

      Jejunum, upper two-fifths.

      Ileum, lower three-fifths.

Appendix, 3 to 4 inches.

Cæcum, 2½ inches.

Ascending colon, 8 inches.

Transverse colon, 20 inches.

Descending colon, 4 to 6 inches.

* The distance from the teeth to the cardiac orifice of the stomach about 16 to 17 inches.

86

Iliac colon, 5 to 6 inches.

Pelvic colon, 16 to 18 inches.

Rectum, 5 to 6 inches.

Anal canal, 1 to $1\frac{1}{2}$ inches.

Femoral canal, $\frac{1}{2}$ inch.

Inguinal canal, $1\frac{1}{2}$ inches.

Cisterna chyli, 1 to 2 inches.

Thoracic duct, 16 to 18 inches.

Kidney, $4\frac{1}{2}$ inches by $2\frac{1}{2}$ inches by $1\frac{1}{2}$ inches.

Ureter, 10 inches.

Male urethra, 8 to 10 inches.

    Prostatic, 1 to $1\frac{1}{2}$ inches.

    Membranous, anterior wall, $\frac{3}{4}$ inch.

        ,,   posterior wall, $\frac{1}{2}$ inch.

    Spongy and penile, 6 to 8 inches.

Testis, $1\frac{1}{2}$ inches by 1 inch by $\frac{3}{4}$ inch.

Seminiferous tubules, 2 to 3 feet.

Canal of the epididymis, 19 to 20 feet.

Vas deferens, 16 to 18 inches.

Ovary, 1 inch by $\frac{1}{2}$ inch.

Uterine (Fallopian) tubes, 4 to $4\frac{1}{2}$ inches.

Uterus, 3 inches by 2 inches by 1 inch.

Vagina, anterior wall, 3 inches.

    ,,   posterior wall, 4 inches.

Female urethra, 1 to $1\frac{1}{2}$ inches.

    1 inch is equivalent to 2.5 centimetres.

THE WEIGHT OF SOME ORGANS.

The brain : Male, 50 ounces ; female, 45 ounces.

The lungs : Together, 42 ounces ; right, 22 ounces ; left, 20 ounces.

The heart : Male, 10 to 12 ounces ; female, 8 to 10 ounces.

The liver, 50 to 60 ounces.

The kidneys, $4\frac{1}{2}$ ounces.

The suprarenals, 1 to 2 drachms.

The prostate, $\frac{3}{4}$ ounce.

The testis, 1 ounce.

The ovary, $\frac{1}{4}$ ounce.

The spinal cord, $1\frac{1}{2}$ ounces.

The pancreas, 2 to 4 ounces.

The spleen, 7 ounces.

1 ounce = 28 grammes.

AN OUTLINE OF THE OSSIFICATION AND EPIPHYSES OF THE SKELETON EXCLUDING THE CRANIUM.

Certain epiphyses and epiphyseal lines have been alluded to in the text, and the following table, compiled from Gray's "Anatomy," Frazer's "The Anatomy of the Human Skeleton," and Cunningham's "Text-book of Anatomy" has consequently been appended :

(a) THE UPPER LIMB :

The Clavicle :

Primary centre :

1 for the shaft (in membrane) in the fourth or fifth week (i.u.l.).*

Secondary centre :

1 centre for the sternal end in the eighteenth to twentieth year.

Union between the two in the twenty-fifth year.

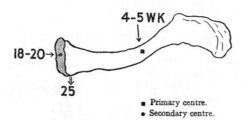

■ Primary centre.
● Secondary centre.

FIG. 30.—CLAVICLE.

The Scapula :

Primary centre :

1 for the body in the eighth week (i.u.l.).

Secondary centres :

1 for the coracoid proper in the first year.

1 for the subcoracoid region (lateral part of the root of the corcaoid and upper one-third of the glenoid cavity) in the tenth year.

Union occurs at puberty.

1 for the margins of the glenoid
1 for the inferior angle
1 for the vertebral border
2 for the acromion
} in the fifteenth year fusing between the twentieth and twenty-fifth years

*i.u.l. = intra-uterine life.

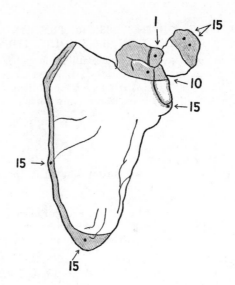

FIG. 31.—SCAPULA.

The Humerus :

Primary centre :

    1 for the shaft in the eighth week (i.u.l.).

Secondary centres :

    1 for the head in the first year.

    1 for the greater tuberosity in the third year.

    1 for the lesser tuberosity in the fifth year.

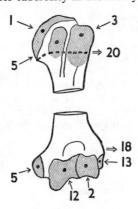

FIG. 32.—HUMERUS.

Head and tuberosities unite in the fifth year, and with the shaft in the twentieth year.

1 for the medial epicondyle in the fifth year.

1 for half the trochlea in the twelfth year.

1 for half the trochlea and capitulum in the second year.

1 for the lateral epicondyle in the thirteenth year.

The last three unite together to form an epiphysis, which unites with the shaft in the seventeenth year, the medial epicondyle joining separately in the eighteenth year.

The Radius and Ulna :

Primary centres :

1 for the shaft of the radius in the eighth week (i.u.l.)

1 for the shaft of the ulna in the eighth week (i.u.l.).

Secondary centres :

1 for the lower end of the radius in the second year.

1 for the lower end of the ulna in the sixth year.

These unite with the shaft in the twentieth year.

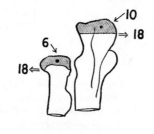

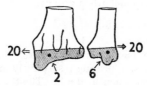

FIG. 33.—RADIUS AND ULNA.

1 for the upper end of the radius in the sixth year.

1 for the upper end of the ulna in the tenth year.

These unite with the shaft in the eighteenth year.

The carpus :

All the bones are cartilaginous at birth. The first centre of ossification appears in the os capitatum and the last in the pisiform. Capitate and hamate, first year—triquetrum, third year—lunate, trapezium and scaphoid, fifth and sixth years—trapezoid, eighth year—pisiform, twelfth year.

The metacarpus and phalanges :

Primary centres :

 1 for the shaft of each metacarpal in the ninth week.

 1 for the shaft of each phalanx between the eighth and the twelfth week.

Secondary centres :

 1 for the head of each metacarpal bone and the base of each phalanx in the third year.

  Union between diaphyses and epiphyses in the twentieth year.

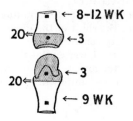

Fig. 34.—Metacarpal and Phalanges.

 The thumb metacarpal is an exception to the rule, a well marked epiphysis always appearing at the base. This bone, therefore, resembles a phalanx in its mode of ossification, though an epiphysis is not infrequently seen in the head of the bone itself.

(b) The Lower Limb :

The os coxæ :

 Three main primary centres for ilium, ischium, and pubis, appearing respectively in the second, third, and fourth months (i.u.l.). The three parts of the bone are separated at first by the Y-shaped acetabular cartilage.

 Five secondary centres appear about puberty for the crest, pubic symphysis, anterior inferior iliac spine, ischial tuberosity, and the acetabular cartilage. These unite at about the twenty-fifth year.

The femur :

Primary centre :

 1 for the shaft in the seventh week (i.u.l.).

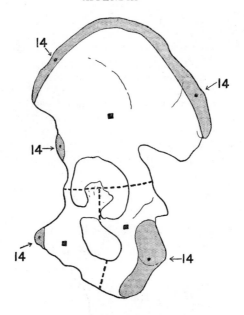

FIG. 35.—Os COXAE.

Secondary centres :
    1 for the head in the first year.
    1 for the greater trochanter in the fourth year.
    1 for the lesser trochanter in the fourteenth year.
        These unite with the shaft in the eighteenth year.
    1 for the lower end in the ninth month (i.u.l.).
        This unites with the shaft in the twentieth year.
The patella :
    1 centre in the third year.
The tibia and fibula :
    Primary centres :
        1 for the shaft of the tibia in the seventh week (i.u.l.).
        1 for the shaft of the fibula in the eighth week (i.u.l.).
    Secondary centres :
        1 for the upper end of the tibia in the first year.
        Union occurs at the twentieth year.
        1 for the upper end of the fibula in the fourth year.
        Union occurs at the twenty-fourth year.
        1 for the lower end of the tibia in the second year
        Union at the eighteenth year.
        1 for the lower end of the fibula in the second year.
        Union at the twenty-first year.

The tarsus :

There are primary centres for each of the tarsal bones.

> 1 for the Calcaneus in the sixth month.
> 1 for the Talus in the eighth month.
> 1 for the Cuboid in the ninth month (at birth).
> 1 for the 3rd Cuneiform in the 1st year.
> 1 each for the Navicular, 1st and 2nd Cuneiforms in the third year.

> The calcaneus possesses a secondary centre for its posterior surface appearing about the tenth year.

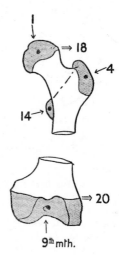

FIG. 36.—FEMUR.

The metatarsus and phalanges :
> The centres appear as in the metacarpus, etc.

The vertebral column :
> There are three primary centres :
>> 1 for the body (starts in the lowest dorsal region and spreads from thence in both directions).
>> 1 for each neural arch (starts at the axis and succeed one another from above downwards).
>> These appear in the seventh week (i.u.l.) and by the third month there are primary centres in all vertebræ.

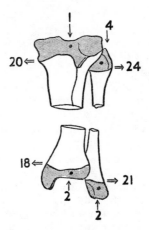

Fig. 37.—Tibia and Fibula.

There are five secondary centres :

 1 for the tip of the spine.
 1 for each of the tips of the transverse processes.
 1 for the upper surface of the body.
 1 for the lower surface of the body.

 These appear at puberty and unite in the twenty-first year.

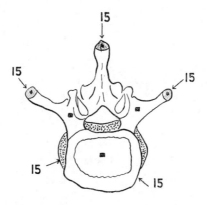

Fig. 38.Vertebra.

The ribs :
    Primary centre :
        1 near the angle in the sixth week (i.u.l.).
    Secondary centres :
        1 for the head   } At puberty and unite in the
        1 for the tubercle   }   twenty-fifth year.

The manubrium and sternum :
    Primary centres :
    The manubrium in the fifth month   } Fuse in
    The sternum   } old age.

        1st segment in the
          sixth month   Twenty-first
        2nd segment in the   year.
          seventh month   Fifteenth
        3rd segment in the   year.
          eighth month
        4th segment in the   Childhood
          ninth month
        Xiphord process in   Middle
          the third year   decade.

The mandible :
    Develops in the first branchial arch, from an ossi-
fication centre in membrane, to the lateral side of
Meckel's cartilage during the sixth week (i.u.l.).
    The two halves fuse in the first year.

INDEX

Abdominal aorta, 61
    planes, 50
Acromion, 20
Adductor tubercle, 75
Aditus to lesser sac (Winslow),
    64
Anatomical snuff-box, 28, 29
Anterior triangle of neck, 13
Aorta, 39
Aortic arch, 39
    intercostals, 41
    valve, 38
Apex beat, 37
Apices of lungs, 46
Appendix, 57
Arcuate line, 52, 62
ARTERIES :
    anterior tibial, 81
    axillary, 29
    brachial, 25, 30
    carotid, 14, 39
    circumflex, posterior, 31
    cœliac, 62
    common iliac, 62
    deep palmar arch, 31
    digitals, 31
    dorsalis pedis, 82
    facial, 15
    femoral, 81
    hepatic, 64
    iliac, 62
    inferior epigastric, 62
        gluteal, 80
        mesenteric, 62
    innominate, 39
    internal mammary, 40
        pudendal, 80
    lingual, 15

    occipital, 15
    plantar, medial and lateral,
      82
    popliteal, 81
    posterior auricular, 15
      tibial, 82
    pulmonary, 40
    radial, 26, 30
    renal, 62
    subclavian, 16, 40
    superficial femoral, 81
      palmar arch, 31
      temporal, 16
    superior gluteal, 80
      mesenteric, 62
      thyroid, 14
    transverse facial, 9
    ulnar, 30
Auricular area of heart, 37
Axilla, 22

Base of the brain, 4
Basic fossæ, 8
Bicipital aponeurosis, 25
    groove, 22
    sulci, 25
Bile-duct, 64
Brain, 4
Bregma, 2
Broca's area, 6
Bronchi, 47
Bryant's triangle and line, 71

Cæcum, 57
Calcaneum, 77
Cardiac dullness, deep, 46
      superficial, 46
    orifice of the stomach, 54

97